Computer Chess

ACM MONOGRAPH SERIES

Published under the auspices of the Association for Computing Machinery Inc.

Editor ROBERT L. ASHENHURST *The University of Chicago*

A. FINERMAN (Ed.) University Education in Computing Science, 1968

A. GINZBURG Algebraic Theory of Automata, 1968

E. F. CODD Cellular Automata, 1968

G. ERNST AND A. NEWELL GPS: A Case Study in Generality and Problem Solving, 1969

M. A. GAVRILOV AND A. D. ZAKREVSKII (Eds.) LYaPAS: A Programming Language for Logic and Coding Algorithms, 1969

THEODOR D. STERLING, EDGAR A. BERING, JR., SEYMOUR V. POLLACK, AND HERBERT VAUGHAN, JR. (Eds.) Visual Prosthesis: The Interdisciplinary Dialogue, 1971

JOHN R. RICE (Ed.) Mathematical Software, 1971

ELLIOTT I. ORGANICK Computer System Organization: The B5700/B6700 Series, 1973

NEIL D. JONES Computability Theory: An Introduction, 1973

ARTO SALOMAA Formal Languages, 1973

HARVEY ABRAMSON Theory and Application of a Bottom-Up Syntax-Directed Translator, 1973

GLEN G. LANGDON, JR. Logic Design: A Review of Theory and Practice, 1974

MONROE NEWBORN Computer Chess, 1975

Previously published and available from The Macmillan Company, New York City

V. KRYLOV Approximate Calculation of Integrals (Translated by A. H. Stroud), 1962

Computer Chess

Monroe Newborn

Department of Electrical Engineering
and Computer Science
Columbia University
New York, New York

ACADEMIC PRESS   New York   San Francisco   London   1975

A Subsidiary of Harcourt Brace Jovanovich, Publishers

ACADEMIC PRESS, INC.
111 Fifth Avenue, New York, New York 10003

United Kingdom Edition published by
ACADEMIC PRESS, INC. (LONDON) LTD.
24/28 Oval Road, London NW1

Library of Congress Cataloging in Publication Data

Newborn, Monroe.
    Computer chess.

    (A.C.M. monograph series)
    Includes bibliographical references and index.
    1.   Electronic data processing–Chess.   2.   Chess
Tournaments.   I.   Title.   II.   Series: Association for
Computing Machinery. ACM monograph series.
GV1318.N48   794.1′7   74-17965
ISBN 0–12–517250–8

Contents

Preface

A digital computer conquered its first human opponent across the chess board in 1956. Since then, the quality of play by computers has improved remarkably and today they are playing on a par with good high school players. Their style of play is quite different from that of humans. There is an obvious lack of long-range planning that becomes glaringly apparent in end-game play. Computers typically look two to four full moves ahead and make moves based on the information gained in the lookahead. If trouble lurks one move beyond the lookahead, it goes undetected. What went undetected on one move may loom up on the next move as does an iceberg before a ship at sea in a fog. Computers do, however, play good tactical chess; to some degree this makes up for their shortcomings in long-range planning.

The aim of this book is twofold: first, to provide the reader with a comprehensive history of computer chess games, and second, to give him an insight into the programming of computer chess. Chapter II presents the historical background of the basic ideas underlying computer chess and several of the earliest games. Chapters III–IX and Appendix I provide a record of the more recent games. The author has been involved in the organization of the four United States Computer Chess Championships and attempts to provide a detailed description of events surrounding these tournaments. Most of the games were played between two computers, but computer versus human games have been included when no other games are available (in the cases of early programs) or when games are of particular significance (Mac Hack Six and KAISSA). Chapter X outlines OSTRICH, a chess program developed by George Arnold and the author.

An individual interested in developing a chess program should be able to do so after digesting the material in Chapters II and X, assuming he has an adequate programming background. About two months of intensive effort are necessary in order to get a minimal working program. There are over forty chess programs in existence today, and the number is increasing rapidly both in the United States and abroad (Norway, Austria, the U.S.S.R., England, Hungary, Switzerland, Germany, and Canada. In the future there may be a library of subprograms available to interested individuals; this should reduce the amount of repeated effort.

For the chess expert, this book will do little to improve his technique. If he has not observed computers at play in the last few years, however, he will be surprised by the quality of the better games. Most exciting is the success of the Soviet program KAISSA in its recent match against the readers of *Komsomolskaia Pravda*, a Russian daily newspaper.

The First, Second, Third, and Fourth United States Computer Chess Championships were part of the Association for Computing Machinery's Annual Conferences of 1970–1973. The Fourth took place recently in Atlanta, Georgia on August 26–28, 1973. These tournaments, hosted by the ACM, and partially supported in the past by the Control Data Corporation, International Business Machines, Sperry–UNIVAC, National Data Industries, and Western Electric, have provided a meeting ground for those interested in computer chess programs and in the broader field of artificial intelligence.

Acknowledgments

The author would like to thank the many people who have offered suggestions and provided help in the preparation of this manuscript. Most particularly, George Arnold, Nadim Habra, Allen Reiter, and Israel Gold have been most willing editors and critics and are due special thanks. The author would also like to thank the Department of Electrical Engineering and Computer Science at Columbia University and the Department of Computer Science at the Technion, Haifa, for providing assistance in the preparation of the manuscript. Finally, a special thanks is extended to Miss Sadie Silverstein for her many hours of patient and gracious help in typing the manuscript.

Grateful acknowledgment is given to the following for permission to quote material as specified:

AFIPS Press, for the listing of moves in one of the computer chess games reported in Greenblatt, R., and Crocker, S., The Greenblatt chess program, *Proc. Fall Joint Computer Conf.*, 801–810, 1967.

Association for Computing Machinery, for the listing of moves and related comments in the computer chess game, the Los Alamos Chess Program versus Beginner, which appears in Kister, J., *et al.*, Experiments in chess, *JACM* **4**, 174–177, 1967, and for other games that appear in issues of the *SIGART Newsletter of the ACM*.

Daphne Productions, for Bobby Fischer's views on computer chess as voiced on the Dick Cavett Television Show, December 21, 1972.

Edinburgh University Press, for the listing of moves in the computer chess game reported in Good, I.J., Analysis of a machine chess game, J. Scott (White), ICL-1900 versus R. D. Greenblatt, PDP-10, *Machine Intelligence*, 267–269, 1969.

W. H. Freeman and Co., for the listing of moves and related comments in the computer chess game that appears in Bernstein, A., and Roberts, M. de V., Computer v. chess player, *Scientific American,* 96–105, June 1958.

IEEE, for the "decision routines" in Bernstein, A., *et al,* A chess playing program for the IBM 704, *Proc. Western Joint Computer Conf.,* 157–159, March 1959.

MIT Press, for extracts from Wiener, N., "Cybernetics," pp. 164, 165 (1948).

Pitman and Sons, Ltd., for the listing of moves and related comments in Turing's chess game reported in Turing, A., Digital computers applied to games, in "Faster Than Thought" (B. V. Bowden, ed.). (1953).

United States Chess Federation, for the listing of moves in the Napoleon versus Turk game, which appears in Harkness, K., and Battell, J., This made chess history, *Chess Rev.,* November 1947.

Computer Chess

CHAPTER I

Introduction

From the very beginning of the development of digital computers, researchers recognized their potential for solving complex problems. They conceived of their use in processing natural languages, in particular, in translating from one language to another. They saw computers being programmed to prove mathematical theorems, to simulate economic systems, to aid in the diagnosis of medical illnesses, to predict the weather, and to design other computers. They even imagined computers programmed to compose music and to write poetry. Many outstanding researchers also touched upon the game of chess.

Chess has many features that make it an excellent problem for those interested in studying how computers might be programmed to solve other complex problems. The rules are well defined, including the definitions of a win, a loss, and a draw. There is no element of chance; all the cards, so to speak, are on the table. It is a game of perfect information. In theory, given enough time, a computer can examine all possible continuations from a given position and can always find the best move to make. However, and here is what makes computer chess an excellent problem, this is usually not possible in practice because of the tremendous number of continuations that exist in most positions. Thus a computer can do little more than selectively search several moves ahead into the tree of all possible continuations using chess *heuristics** to guide the search. It must

---

* A chess *heuristic* might be defined as a chess *rule of thumb*. For example, one chess heuristic is this: avoid moving the King from the first rank early in the game. In general, this is a good policy, but there are times when it is best to move the King from the back row early in the game. This heuristic, like most others, is dangerous to follow with absolute faith.

1

decide which move to make based on this nearsighted look-ahead. A move is said to be determined by a finite-depth *heuristic tree-searching procedure.* Most programs that do language processing, theorem proving, medical diagnosis, and computer circuit design include heuristic tree-searching procedures. And while a chess program is similar in structure to these programs, it has one particularly convenient feature: one can obtain a fairly accurate measure of a program's strength by pitting it against human opponents—or against other computers—of known strength.*

Over the last twenty years computer chess programs have been written, and games pitting computer versus man and computer versus computer have been played. The best programs presently play at a level of mediocre club players or at the level of good high school players. The newer programs are better than the old, with the improvement primarily due to advances in computer hardware and software and to more thorough programming efforts rather than to any new fundamental breakthroughs in how to program computers to play better. Due to hardware advances, today's computers are several hundred times faster than they were when chess programs were first written. Software advances make the editing and debugging of programs orders of magnitude easier than it was at first.

Bobby Fischer had the following to say when asked about the possibilities of computer chess on the Dick Cavett Television Show on December 21, 1972:

> Yes, I believe that it is possible (in principle) for me to be beaten by a computer. . . But they have a long way to go. They're only playing at the class B level, which is five or six levels below me. And up to now they've only had computer scientists developing such programs, and they won't go anywhere until they actually involve some good chess players.

Fischer was well aware of the level of play by computers (and even may have been a little charitable), but he was a bit unfair when he implied that no good chess players were involved. Some of the best chess players in the United States are involved, as well as one former world champion from the Soviet Union.

The most outstanding chess player in the United States to have written a chess program so far is Hans Berliner. Berliner was World Correspondence Chess Champion several years ago. He is presently a doctoral student at Carnegie-Mellon University in Pittsburgh in the field of computer science. David Slate, rated an expert by the USCF, has been behind the Northwestern University program, which has won the United States Com-

---

* Most good chess players in the USA have United States Chess Federation (USCF) ratings, as do several computers.

puter Chess Championship for the last four years. Charles Kalme, one of the top fifty chess players in the United States, has been assisting a group at the University of Southern California. In the Soviet Union, Mikhail Botvinnik, world champion from 1948 to 1963 (with the exceptions of 1957 and 1960 when Vassily Smyslov and Mikhail Tal were champions, respectively), has been developing a chess program for several years with the help of a colleague, V. Butenko, based on ideas presented in his book "Computers, Chess, and Long-Range Planning."

That no program presently plays at the Master level is not at all surprising to anyone closely involved. On the other hand, the prospects for the future look quite good. No presently functioning program has been in existence for more than six years. A minimum of fifteen years of intensive work by an excellent programer and chess player seems necessary to write a program that might compete with Masters. Many hours of programming and many hours of observation and analysis of the resulting play are required. Additionally, there will be several developments that should make the task easier. The computers of tomorrow will be much faster than present ones; a speedup by a factor of several hundred in the next fifteen years is not too unreasonable to expect. This will allow much larger move trees to be searched. Chess programs of the future will also make use of very large files of stored book openings, which will allow computers to play each of the first ten to fifteen moves of a game in a matter of several seconds, leaving more time for the complex middle game. Special endgame programs will also be developed by one individual or group and will be made available to other groups.* Thus, with fifteen years of work by someone who is an outstanding chess player and programmer and with computers several hundred times faster than they are today, and with the sharing of special programs, it seems quite possible to develop a chess program that will compete on an even footing with a Master without any new breakthroughs in the field.

What will happen to the game of chess if and when computers are capable of playing on a level with Masters, or even perhaps on a level with Bobby Fischer, as he himself concedes is possible? Will the game die? Will people lose interest? No, that will not happen. Instead, a new era in the history of chess will emerge, an era in which the game is not playing chess but programming computers to play. Programs will have their own individal "personalities" and will reflect the chess styles of their authors. This revolution in the chess world lies somewhere in the future— the new game will be far more exciting than the old!

* See, for example, Barbara J. Huberman, "A Program to Play Chess End Games," Stanford Univ. Tech. Rept. CS 106, August 19, 1968.

References

The reader who would like to learn more about research activities on subjects closely related to computer chess is encouraged to seek out the references listed below:

Machine Intelligence (Bernard Meltzer and Donald Michie, eds.). Edinburgh at the University Press, Edinburgh. [Published yearly since 1965.]

Artificial Intelligence (Bernard Meltzer and Bertram Raphael, eds.). North-Holland, Amsterdam. [Published quarterly since 1969.]

Computers and the Humanities (Joseph Raben, ed.). Queens College Press, Flushing, New York. [Published since 1966.]

Feigenbaum, E. A., and Feldman, J. (eds.), "Computers and Thought." McGraw-Hill, New York (1967).

Chomsky, Noam, "Language and Mind." Harcourt, New York (1968).

Nilsson, Nils, "Problem Solving Methods in Artificial Intelligence." McGraw-Hill, New York (1971). [This book can serve as a text for a one-semester course on the subject of artificial intelligence.]

Reichardt, Jasia (ed.), "Cybernetics, Art, and Ideas." New York Graphic Society, Greenwich, Connecticut (1971).

Slagle, James, "Artificial Intelligence, the Heuristic Programming Approach." McGraw-Hill, New York (1971).

Solomonoff, R. Some recent work in artificial intelligence, *Proc. IEEE* **54**, 1687–1697, December (1966).

CHAPTER II

The History and Basic Ideas of Computer Chess

Two hundred years ago, before magic and mysticism had yet yielded to logic and reason, Baron Wolfgang von Kempelen constructed the first chess automaton, calling it the Turk [1]. The project began in 1769. When it was completed the following year, the Baron exhibited it in the court of the Austrian Empress Maria Theresa. It looked like a large desk with a chessboard on its top. The humanlike figure of the Turk was attached to the automaton, positioned as if to watch over the board. Inside the structure there was enough space for a chess player to hide and to operate mechanisms necessary for moving pieces on the chessboard. Before the start of a game its doors were opened, revealing fake mechanical gears. Meanwhile, the concealed individual maneuvered from one position to another in order to stay hidden from view. The audience was thus led to believe that the automaton was a purely mechanical device. When they subsequently observed that it played an excellent game of chess, they were left in awe!

The Turk was exhibited by von Kempelen in several European cities. Upon his death in 1804, it was bought by John Maelzel. In 1809, Napoleon matched wits with the Turk and was soundly trounced [2]. The loss so enraged Napoleon that, after the game was over, he knocked the pieces off the board. The Turk came to America in 1827 and toured for eleven years. One of America's top chess players, Schlumberger, hid inside during those years. Both Maelzel and Schlumberger died in 1838. The Turk was retired to the Philadelphia Chinese Museum in 1840 where it remained relatively unnoticed in a corner. On July 5, 1854, it was destroyed by a fire in the museum.

The Turk toured for seventy years and participated in hundreds of exhibitions. Besides Napoleon, it had attracted the attention of Benjamin Franklin [3] and Edgar Allan Poe [4]. Poe and Robert Willis [5] had speculated correctly on the Turk's secret, which was revealed in Baltimore on June 1, 1827, after two boys had observed Schlumberger exit from the automaton behind stage on a hot day in May. Their story was published in the *Baltimore Gazette* but was discounted by other newspapers, which evidently were satisfied with the authenticity of the Turk and felt the Baltimore story was a publicity gimmick [6]!

Around this same time, at least four other chess automatons were built. Baron von Racknitz built a sequel to the Turk in Germany in 1789, and the Walker brothers built and exhibited another in New York in May 1827 [1]. The other two automatons were built in England: "Ajeeb" was the work of Charles Arthur Hopper (1868), and "Mephisto" was invented by Charles Godfrey Gumpel (1878) [7].

The following is a listing of the moves of the Napoleon–Turk game. Napoleon went for a quick kill but found himself on the defensive after the sixth move! His Queen fell on the fourteenth move. The game lasted five more moves, ending with Napoleon in a hopeless position.

WHITE: *Napoleon*   BLACK: *Turk*

1 P–K4	P–K4	11 B–N3	N × P (R6)+
2 Q–B3	N–QB3	12 K–R2	Q–R5
3 B–B4	N–B3	13 P–N3	N–B6+
4 N–K2	B–B4	14 K–N2	N × Q+
5 P–QR3	P–Q3	15 R × N	Q–N5
6 O–O	B–KN5	16 P–Q3	B × P(B7)
7 Q–Q3	N–KR4	17 R–R1	Q × P(N6)+
8 P–R3	B × N	18 K–B1	B–Q5
9 Q × B	N–B5	19 K–K2	. . .
10 Q–K1	N–Q5		

The subject of computer chess was discussed by Charles Babbage in 1864. Babbage, the inventor of the analytical engine, the mechanical forerunner of the modern electronic digital computer, was evidently a student of the game of chess, and he speculated on how his analytical engine might play. He noted that "every game of skill is susceptible of being played by an automaton." However, his ideas on how an automaton might play chess were quite vague and naive. He wrote that "the whole question of making an automaton play any game depended upon the possibility of the machine being able to represent all the myriads of combinations relating to it (the game)," and concluded that his analytical engine was capable of playing chess. But instead of going on to describe how it might be done, he chose to explain how an analytical engine might play tic-tac-toe—a somewhat easier task [8]!

Coinciding with the early development of electronic computers, several leading cyberneticists became interested in chess. In 1944, John von Neumann and Oskar Morgenstern studied the general theory of games. They presented the minimax algorithm and showed how it applied, in theory, to the game of chess [9]. They said that a chess game could not continue indefinitely because of the "tie rule," which says: "If no Pawn has been moved and no officer taken for 40* moves, then play is terminated by a tie." This implies that in any chess position if a player could "see" far enough ahead, he would be able to decide whether his present position is a win, a loss, or a draw. He could then always make the best move. Since this could be done in any position, there is no reason why it could not be done in the initial position. That is, in theory at least, the first player to move can determine whether he is able to win or draw or is forced to lose. They went on to say that there is

> no practically usable method to determine the best move. This . . . difficulty necessitates the use of those incomplete, heuristic methods of playing, which constitute "good" chess. . . .

In his book, "Cybernetics" [10], Norbert Wiener discusses briefly how computers might play chess. Wiener was interested in the question of "whether it is possible to construct a chess-playing machine, and whether this sort of ability represents an essential difference between the potentials of the machine and the mind." He realized that it was impossible

> to construct a machine which will play an optimum game in the sense of von Neumann . . . (but that) it is unquestionably possible to construct a machine that will play chess in the sense of following the rules of the game, irrespective of the merit of the play.

He was more interested in the intermediate problem: whether it is possible "to construct a machine which shall offer interesting opposition to a player at some one of the many levels at which human chess players find themselves." He felt that this was clearly possible.

> The machine must actually play—at a high speed if possible—all its own moves and all the opponent's admissible ripostes for two or three moves ahead. To each *sequence of moves* it should assign a certain conventional valuation

and select the move to make using von Neumann's minimax algorithm (which will be explained shortly). Wiener says that

---

* An error by von Neumann and Morgenstern. The rules of chess specify 50 moves, rather than 40.

to checkmate the opponent receives the highest valuation at each stage, to be checkmated the lowest; while losing pieces, taking opponent's pieces, checking, and other recognizable situations should receive valuations not too remote from those which good players would assign them.

Wiener concludes that

such a machine would not only play legal chess, but a chess not so manifestly bad as to be ridiculous . . . It would probably win over a stupid or careless chess player, and would almost certainly lose to a careful player of any considerable degree of proficiency.

The machine could "attain a pretty fair level of accomplishment."

However, Claude Shannon in 1950 published what has become recognized as the fundamental paper on computer chess [11]. Shannon never wrote a chess program, but his paper outlines a procedure that could be implemented by a computer programmer. All the chess programs that have ever been written and that are of any significance today are based on Shannon's ideas. Actually Shannon's paper proposes two different procedures; the second procedure is an extension of the first. Shannon wrote his paper while he was a researcher at Bell Telephone Laboratories, Murray Hill, New Jersey. Presently he is on the faculty of the electrical engineering department at MIT. His contributions to the world of cybernetics are numerous and include the discovery of basic concepts related to the design of computer circuits and to the field of communication theory.

Shannon's Contribution

Shannon's paper begins by reminding the reader of von Neumann and Morgenstern's work. Shannon indicates that the rule requiring a Pawn advance or a capture every fifty moves places an upper bound on the maximum number of moves that a game may last: 6350 moves. He calculates that there are 10^{120} different sequences of moves that begin with the initial position. He indicates that an extremely fast computer would require more than 10^{90} years to examine them and then to select its first move! He concludes, as did von Neumann and Morgenstern, that this approach is impractical, and then he goes on to outline a procedure that a computer could follow. He suggests that the computer select a move in a given position by using chess *strategy* in somewhat the same way as did Wiener.

In order to illustrate the idea of using a strategy to select a move in a given position, Shannon proposes two trivial possibilities: (1) form a list of all legal moves and select the move at the top; (2) form a list of all legal moves and select one of them by random means. These two strategies obviously provide a very weak level of play. Shannon then presents a feasible strategy, one that might allow the computer to play with some degree of proficiency, which depends on two concepts: (1) the scoring of a position,* and (2) the minimax algorithm. We will first review his ideas on the scoring of a position and then go on to describe the minimax algorithm.

Any chess player can look at a chessboard and conclude whether the position is good or bad for one side or the other. The better the player, the more accurate the assessment. One might argue that the better player probably considers more "factors" when evaluating or *scoring* a position and probably breaks each factor down into finer gradations. Shannon suggests that a computer score a position in the same way. He specifies three factors that should be considered and recommends that they be assigned numerical values as follows:

(1) *Material.* Material is most often the dominant factor in evaluating a position. The pieces should be valued as follows: Queen=9, Rook=5, Bishop=3, Knight=3, Pawn=1, and King=200. The King is more valuable than all the other pieces.

(2) *Pawn structure.* One should usually avoid doubled, backward, and isolated Pawns. Thus for each doubled, backward, and isolated Pawn, Shannon suggests a 0.5-point penalty.

(3) *Mobility.* One generally wants his pieces to have good mobility while keeping the opponent's pieces cramped. Thus Shannon recommends a 0.1-point bonus for each legal move that a side has available.

The score S of a position P, denoted by $S(P)$, is then given by the *scoring function*

$$S(P) = 200(K-K') + 9(Q-Q') + 5(R-R') + 3(B-B'+N-N')$$
$$+ (P-P') - 0.5(D-D'+S-S'+I-I') + 0.1(M-M')$$

where K, Q, R, B, N, and P are the number of White Kings, Queens, Rooks, Bishops, Knights, and Pawns; D, S, and I represent doubled, backward, and isolated Pawns; M is the number of legal moves for White. Primed variables represent similar variables for Black. A positive score implies that White is ahead while a negative one implies that Black is ahead.

Six positions and their Shannon scores are shown in Fig. II-1. Figure II-1a shows that the initial board position has a score of 0 as does any other symmetric position. Figures II-1b (score of +1.0) and II-1c (score of +0.8) indicate that White's first move P–K4 leads to a position with a better score than does P–Q4. Figures II-1d and II-1e show that a score

---

* Shannon assigned scores to positions; Wiener leaves the reader in some doubt whether moves or positions are to be scored.

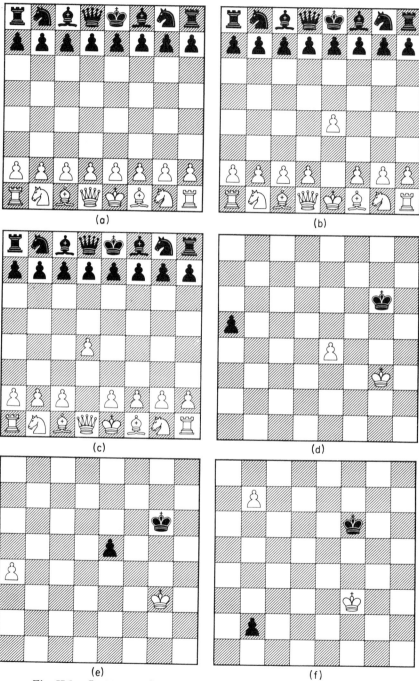

Fig. II-1. *Positions and scores illustrating Shannon's scoring function.*

can be misleading. Both figures have identical scores (0) but Fig. II-1d is a won position for Black while Fig. II-1e is a won position for White. Finally, in Fig. II-1f, the score is again misleading; although the score is 0, indicating an even game, if it is White's turn to move, he can win, while if it is Black's turn to move, he can win!

Shannon indicates that the scoring function has only a "statistical validity" and, as we have seen, can be misleading in many cases, particularly in the end game. The appendix to his paper proposes several other terms that could be included in the scoring function. The reader is encouraged to design such a function for himself. In Chapter X, we examine the scoring function of a specific program.

Based on the scoring function, Shannon next defines a "one-move look-ahead strategy" for selecting a move in a given position. Calculate (or, as is usually said, generate) all legal moves for the side to move in position P. Call them $M_1, M_2, \ldots, M_r$. Next, for each move construct the new position that follows. Call these new positions $M_1P, M_2P, \ldots, M_rP$. Then calculate the score of each of these positions. Call them $S(M_1P)$, $S(M_2P), \ldots, S(M_rP)$. Finally, if it is White's turn to move, select the move that leads to the position with the highest or *maximum* score. If it is Black's turn, select the move that leads to the position with the lowest or *minimum* score.

The *tree* in Fig. II-2 illustrates this strategy for a hypothetical position P having four legal moves for White, M_1, M_2, M_3, and M_4. The *node* at the left represents position P and is called the *root* of the tree. The four moves are represented by *branches* connecting the root node on the left to the *terminal nodes* on the right. The terminal nodes represent positions M_1P, M_2P, M_3P, and M_4P. The score of each terminal node is shown beside it. By looking ahead one move, or one *ply*, the figure indicates that White's best move is M_2, which leads to a position with a score of +14.

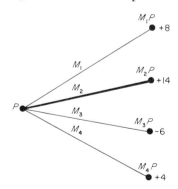

Fig. II-2.   *A move tree.*

Accordingly, we say that position P can be assigned a *backed-up score* of $+14$; that is, $S_B(P)=+14$. More generally, in any position P, White moves in such a way that the backed-up score of position P is *maximum*. Similarly, Black always moves in such a way that the backed-up score is *minimum*. In mathematical terms, we say that White selects the move for which $S_B(P) = \max_i S(M_iP)$, while Black selects the move for which $S_B(P) = \min_i S(M_iP)$.

Shannon next defines a "two-move look-ahead strategy" as follows. Generate all legal moves for White (assuming White's turn to move) in position P. Call them $M_1, M_2, \ldots, M_r$. Next construct nonterminal positions $M_1P, M_2P, \ldots, M_rP$ and then apply Shannon's one-move strategy for Black to move in each of these positions. This will give (1) Black's best move and (2) the corresponding backed-up score for each of the positions $M_1P, M_2P, \ldots, M_rP$. Finally, based on the backed-up scores for the nonterminal positions $M_1P, M_2P, \ldots, M_rP$, apply Shannon's one-move look-ahead strategy for White to move in position P.

For example, consider the two-ply tree shown in Fig. II-3. Three moves can be made in position P leading to positions M_1P, M_2P, and M_3P. In each of these three positions, there are also three moves. We say that

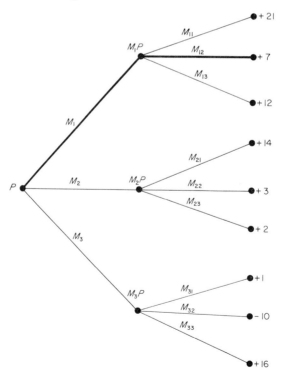

Fig. II-3. *A tree of depth 2. The principal continuation is heavily shaded.*

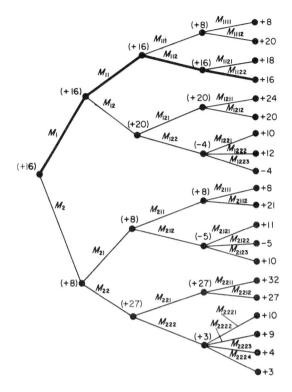

Fig. II-4. *A tree of depth 4. The principal continuation is heavily shaded.*

the *fanout* of each node in this tree is three. The scores indicate that Black's best move in position M_1P is move M_{12} and that the backed-up score of node M_1P is +7. In position M_2P, Black's best move is M_{23}, and the corresponding backed-up score of position M_2P is +2. In position M_3P, Black's best move is M_{32}, and the backed-up score of position M_3P is −10. These scores imply that White's best move at ply 1 is M_1, and that the backed-up score of position P is +7. We say that move M_1 followed by move M_{12} constitutes the *principal continuation*, the sequence of moves that the two-ply look-ahead strategy calculates will be made if each side is attempting to reach the best possible position for itself. In general, using Shannon's two-move look-ahead strategy, White selects the move at ply 1 that leads to the position with the maximum of the minimum scores selected by Black at ply 2. We say that White looks ahead two moves and uses the *minimax algorithm* to determine which move to make.

Shannon went on to generalize the one- and two-move look-ahead strategies to the *type-A strategy*. In the type-A strategy all sequences of moves are generated to some fixed depth and then the move to be made is determined by backing up scores from the terminal nodes to the root node using the obvious generalization of the minimax algorithm.

Figure II-4 presents an example of Shannon's type-A strategy when applied to a tree of depth 4. The backed-up scores of all nonterminal nodes are shown in parentheses. The backed-up score of the root node is $+16$ and the principal continuation is $M_1 M_{11} M_{112} M_{1122}$.

Shannon's type-A strategy has some serious weaknesses. First, one cannot examine even a moderately deep tree in a practical amount of time. In a typical chess position there are around 30 to 35 legal moves. If one were to use the type-A strategy with a 4-ply look-ahead, there would be about 1,000,000 terminal positions that must be scored and about 30,000 nonterminal positions at which all legal moves must be generated. If one assumes a position can be scored in 10 μsec and that a move generation requires 1 msec (these figures are well less than one-tenth the amount of time required by most current chess programs!), then a move would require 40 sec. The type-A strategy with a 6-ply look-ahead would consume about 1000×40 sec or about 11 hours per move! Thus it is clearly impossible to look ahead more than four ply. The second major shortcoming is that all variations are evaluated to *exactly* some fixed depth. Most good human players search a tree of moves in which most variations are considered only for a move or two while the more interesting variations and the forced variations are examined to much greater depths. A fixed-depth search often might lead to trouble. For example, if the move at the last ply were a capture, one would certainly want to see whether the opponent could recapture or answer with an equally good move move before necessarily concluding that the capture was a good move. This led Shannon to propose the *type-B-strategy*—a variable depth of search strategy:

Explore all sequences of moves to some arbitrary depth, say 4 ply. Score a position at this ply unless the position warrants deeper search because of en prise pieces on the board, etc. Search if necessary to some arbitrary depth (he suggests 20 ply).

Shannon adds that the type-B strategy could be further improved by using *forward pruning*. At each node in the tree, he suggests that the computer give all moves a preliminary examination or screening and select only a small subset of them for further study. At positions near the root of the tree the screening would eliminate fewer moves than it would at positions at deeper ply. The screening would eliminate moves that are "obviously bad," a task that is easier said than done!

Shannon's paper discusses the design of a chess program. He suggests that the program for carrying out the type-A strategy consist of nine subprograms. He assumes that there exists a supervisory program that handles the input and output of moves. His nine subprograms are:

(1) a routine to make a move in position P to obtain a new position;

(2) a routine to generate a list of moves for each piece: Pawn, Knight, Bishop, Rook, Queen, and King;

.
.
.

(7) a routine to determine an overall list of possible moves in a given position;

(8) a routine to calculate the score of a position;

(9) a routine for searching the tree looking for the principal continuation based on the minimax algorithm.

Shannon points out that a large memory is not necessary to store the data gathered during the search. At any given time in the search of a tree of depth n, it is necessary to store only the *one* position under current examination along with n lists of legal moves, one list for each ply in the tree. In order to generate new positions or return to old ones, the computer simply updates and restores the single stored position. This function requires a small amount of memory. Shannon concludes that his program needs only 3000 bits. Most chess programs in existence today, being considerably more complex than the one Shannon proposes, occupy around 10,000 to 20,000 words, where a word contains somewhere between 16 and 60 bits.

Turing and a Hand Simulation of a Chess Program [*]

Paralleling the work of Shannon, Alan Turing, of the University of Manchester in England, published his approach to the automation of chess strategy. Turing, like Shannon, is one of the outstanding names in the history of computers. He established important fundamental theorems regarding the computational capabilities of digital computers. His research also includes the area of numerical analysis. Turing was quite interested in computer chess and his ideas were very similar to Shannon's. He can be credited with having played (and published) the first "computer chess" game.

Turing's paper suggests the use of a scoring function and the minimax algorithm, as does Shannon's, although Turing's scoring function is much simpler having material as the only factor. If two or more moves at ply 1, say $M_1, M_2, \ldots, M_p$, are found to have identical scores, an additional calculation is carried out to break the tie. This calculation deter-

[*] See Turing [12].

mines a positional value for each of the new positions $M_1P, M_2P, \ldots, M_pP$ yielded by these moves. The move leading to the position having the highest positional value is selected. The positional value is calculated using only the pieces of the side to move (P, N, B, R, Q, K) and the opponent's King ($-K$):

(1) *Mobility.* For the Q,R,B,N, add the square root of the number of moves the piece can make; count each capture as two moves.

(2) *Piece safety.* For the R,B,N, add 1.0 point if it is defended, and 1.5 points if it is defended at least twice.

(3) *King mobility.* For the K, the same as (1) except for castling moves.

(4) *King safety.* For the K, deduct points for its vulnerability as follows: assume that a Queen of the same color is on the King's square; calculate its mobility, and then subtract this value from the score.

(5) *Castling.* Add 1.0 point for the possibility of still being able to castle on a later move if a King or Rook move is being considered; add another point if castling can take place on the next move; finally add one more point for actually castling.

(6) *Pawn credit.* Add 0.2 point for each rank advanced, and 0.3 point for being defended by a non-Pawn.

(7) *Mates and checks.* Add 1.0 point for the threat of mate and 0.5 point for a check.

Turing assigns slightly different values to the pieces than does Shannon: Pawn = 1, Knight = 3, Bishop = 3.5, Rook = 5, and Queen = 10.

A search strategy similar to Shannon's type-B strategy was set forth. Turing specifies examining all moves for two plies and then examining only *considerable moves* at deeper plies, stopping when a *dead position* is reached. He defines a considerable move as (1) a recapturing move, (2) the capture of an undefended piece, (3) the capture of a piece of higher value by one of lower value, and (4) a move giving checkmate. A dead position is a position in which there are no considerable moves.

Turing's paper presents a game that he played against a very weak human opponent who was unaware of his strategy. Turing calculated his own moves by hand. He simplified the square roots of the integers to the following values:

Number:	0	1	2	3	4	5	6	7	8	9	10	11	12	13
Square Root:	0	1	1.4	1.7	2.0	2.2	2.4	2.6	2.8	3.0	3.2	3.3	3.5	3.6

The game is presented below. The change in positional value due to the move selected is shown in parentheses, following the move, when relevant.

Turing's Game (1951)

WHITE: *Turing's hand simulation*   BLACK: *Human opponent*

| 1 P–K4 (4.2) | P–K4 | 3 P–Q4 (2.6) | B–N5 |
| 2 N–QB3 (3.1) | N–KB3 | 4 N–B3 (2.0) | . . . |

Turing reminds the reader that, even though 4 B–Q2 has a higher positional score, it is rejected because the two-ply calculation indicates that 4 . . . , P × P loses material.

| 4 . . . | P–Q3 | 6 P–Q5 (0.2) | N–Q5 |
| 5 B–Q2 (3.5) | N–B3 | 7 P–KR4 (1.1) | . . . |

Turing's algorithm results in Pawn advances when there is no immediate tactical threat. For 7 P–KR4, the mobility of the Rook increases and credit is given for Pawn advancement. This type of move will be seen many times in the games in later chapters, although somewhat less often in the better games.

| 7 . . . | B–N5 | 8 P–R4 (1.0) . . . |

This move is made for the same reason as White's last.

| 8 . . . | N × N+ | 10 B–QN5+ (2.4) | . . . |
| 9 P × N | B–KR4 | | |

(See Fig. II-5.) Programs are prone to check whenever possible. In this case, however, the checking move is reasonable. At first glance, it seems

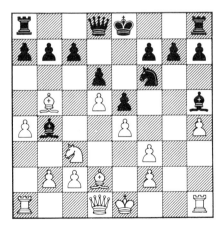

Fig. II-5.   *Position after 10 B–QN5+.*

that Black can play 10 . . . , P–B3, chasing the Bishop away, but this is not the best as we will see. Better for Black is 10 . . . , N–Q2. Black's 8 . . . , N × N+ takes the pressure off White temporarily.

10 . . .	P–B3	13 B–QR6 (−1.5)	Q–R4
11 P × P	O–O	14 Q–K2 (0.6)	N–Q2
12 P × P	R–N1		

Black overlooked 14 . . . , B × P; 15 Q × B, Q × B; etc.

| 15 R–KN1 (1.2) | N–B4 | 16 R–N5 | . . . |

Turing states "Heads in the sand!" The program behaves like an ostrich! White stalls the inevitable loss of its Knight's Pawn by harassing the Bishop. This Bishop can make a safe retreat and White will be left with its original problem. White has simply avoided looking at its real problem. The move 16 R–N5 forces the loss of material to occur no earlier than the fourth ply [17 . . . , N × P(N2)]; the program does not see that far ahead.

| 16 . . . | B–N3 | 18 O–O–O (3.2) | . . . |
| 17 B–N5 (0.4) | N × P(N2) | | |

The Queen-side castling move receives a very high score. Programs give high priority to castling and often castle to the wrong side.

18 . . .	N–B4	24 Q–Q3	N–N4
19 B–B6	R(B1)–B1	25 B–N3	Q–R3
20 B–Q5	B × N	26 B–B4	B–R4
21 B × B (0.7)	Q × P	27 R–N3	Q–R5
22 K–Q2	N–K3	28 B × N	Q × B
23 R–N4 (−0.3)	N–Q5	29 Q × P	. . .

(See Fig. II-6.) "Fiddling while Rome burns," Turing states. White does not search deeply enough to see that Black's 29 . . . , R–Q1 leads to the loss of a Queen for a Rook.

| 29 . . . | R–Q1 | 30 Resigns |

The Los Alamos Chess Program (1957) *

The ideas advanced by Shannon and Turing were first put to a test by several groups in the late 1950s. The Los Alamos group of James

* See Kister *et al.* [13].

Kister, Paul Stein, Stanislaw Ulam, William Walden, and Mark Wells was first to report its work in 1957. Their program was written for the MANIAC I, a UNIVAC computer, located at the Los Alamos Scientific Laboratory. Kister, Walden, and Wells did the majority of the programming work and received consultation from Stein and Ulam. Computers were in their infancy in those days and were designed using unreliable vacuum tubes. The MANIAC I was about 100 times slower than the computers presently available, typically executing 11,000 instructions per second. The software that was available was also much cruder than today; operating systems for computers had not yet been developed. To write a chess program in those days must have been a very nerve-wracking experience.

The Los Alamos group decided that it was necessary to write a program to play "miniature chess" rather than the usual game if moves were to be made in a reasonable period of time. Miniature chess is played on a 6 × 6 board, without Bishops, and with six Pawns per side. Pawns are allowed to move only one square at a time. Pawn promotions are made according to the usual rules. By playing this simpler game their program is able to examine all moves to a depth of four ply and make a move in about 12 minutes. They state that in the usual position there are about 20 legal moves (although a playthrough of their published game indicates the number is closer to 15).

Material and mobility are the only two factors included in the scoring function. Each legal move is given a weight of one-eighth of a Pawn.

The authors of the Los Alamos program report three games that the program played. The first game pitted the program against itself. In the second, the program played against Dr. Martin Kruskal, a mathematician

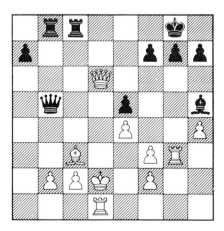

Fig. II-6.   *Position after 29 Q × P.*

and strong chess player, who spotted the computer a Queen while taking White for himself. The authors state that "after about 15 moves Kruskal had made no gain and had even started calling his opponent *he* instead of *it*." (This is a common experience in man–computer games. After perhaps 10–15 moves, humans often begin to carry on a dialogue with the computer, addressing it as *he*, telling it to hurry up, and asking questions such as "What do you think of my last move?" When one human plays another, the feelings of the two players are communicated quite subtly. When playing a computer a human is often eager to express his thoughts and emotions; frequently a strange hostility develops.) After several more moves, however, the program "played a weak continuation which enabled the opponent to lay a three-move mating trap." The program's only way to avoid mate required sacrificing its Queen; the end came on the thirty-eighth move. The authors did not publish either of these two games.

The third game matched the program against a human opponent who had been taught the game during the previous week. She had been coached explicitly for the purpose of seeing how well the program could do against a beginner. The program won! The game and the authors' comments follow:

The Los Alamos CP versus Beginner, 1956

WHITE: *Los Alamos CP*   BLACK: *Beginner*

1 P–K3	P–QN3	4 N–N1	P–QR3
2 N–KR3	P–K3	5 P × P(R4)	. . .
3 P–QN3	P–N3		

"A strategic error; isolating White's Queen's Rook's Pawn and allowing Black's Knight out could prove fatal." (See Fig. II-7.)

5 . . .	N × P	6 K–K2	. . .

"Could lead to a lost game if Black should play P–Q3."

6 . . .	N–Q4

"Whew!"

7 N × N	P(N3) × N+

"A weak move giving White a passed Pawn. P(K3) × N+ is forced."

8 K–K1	P–R3	9 P–QR3	R–N1

"Pointless, as Black takes it back on the next move."

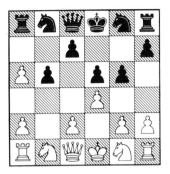

Fig. II-7. *Position after 5 P × P(R4).*

10 P–R4	R–R1	13 Q–R2+	K–N2
11 P–R5	K–K2	14 R–N1	. . .
12 Q–R3	Q–N2		

"Needlessly giving up a Pawn. MANIAC I growing overconfident?" (See Fig. II–8.)

14 . . .	R × P	16 R–N1	R–QR2
15 R × Q	R × Q		

"A timid move. Black should hold on to the fifth rank."

17 P–R3   R–R3

"Compounding the error. White gets a Pawn free. P–N4 was imperative."

18 P(R3) × P   P–Q3

"Allows a quick finish, as MANIAC I mercilessly demonstrates."

19 N–R3+   K–K1   20 P–N5+   . . .

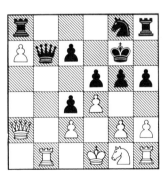

Fig. II-8. *Position after 14 R–N1.*

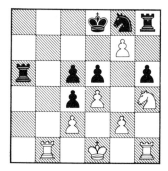

Fig. II-9. *Position after 20 P–N5+.*

(See Fig. II-9.)

| 20 . . . | K–K2 | 22 Q × P(K4)+ | K–Q1 |
| 21 P × R = Q | N–Q2 | 23 N–N5 mate | |

The Bernstein Chess Program (1958) *

The first full-fledged chess program was reported in 1958 and was the work of Alex Bernstein, Michael de V. Roberts, Thomas Arbuckle, and Martin A. Belsky. The program was written for the IBM 704, one of the last in the series of IBM's vacuum-tube computers. The authors say that the program searches a tree of move sequences to a depth of four ply. Forward pruning is performed at each node and the program considers only the 7 most plausible moves in each position for further examination. This implies that moves are generated in a total of $1 + 7 + 49 + 343 = 400$ positions, while $7^4 = 2401$ positions are scored. The selective search results in an examination of about 2.4% of the terminal positions—a relatively narrow search. A move typically required 8 minutes. The IBM 704 executes about 42,000 instructions per second; if one assumes eight times as many instructions are executed at a nonterminal node as at a terminal node, then about 28,800 instructions are executed at each nonterminal node and 3600 instructions at each terminal node.

The authors' scoring function includes four factors: (1) mobility, (2) area control, (3) King defense, and (4) material. Material far outweighs the other three factors; the scoring function never recommends a move that results in the loss of material in return for a gain in the other factors. Mobility is determined by calculating the number of moves avail-

* See Bernstein *et al.* [14], and Bernstein and Roberts [15].

able to each side. Area control involves the number of squares under control by each side, with increased credit being given for the control of center squares. King defense depends on control of squares adjacent to the King.

The forward pruning of the tree is accomplished by "decision routines." The program selects seven moves at each node by asking the following set of questions [14]:

(1) Is the King in check?

(2) a. Can material be gained? b. Can material be lost? c. Can material be exchanged?

(3) Is castling possible?

(4) Can minor pieces be developed?

(5) Can key squares be occupied? (Key squares are those squares controlled by diagonally connected Pawns.)

(6) Can open files be occupied?

(7) Can any Pawns be moved?

(8) Can any piece be moved?

At each node in the tree the program sequentially scans this list of questions. Whenever a question is answered in the affirmative, the moves relevant to the question are added to the plausible moves list for that position. The program stops looking for moves after seven plausible moves have been found or after a castling move has been added to the list.

In the *Scientific American* [15] of June 1958, the authors report a game played between their program and a "skillful opponent." The game lasted 23 moves, although there is little question about the outcome after move 12. The Bernstein CP erred by trading away a well-placed Bishop on move 5 and by failing to develop its Queen's Knight on move 7. The game and the authors' comments follow [15]:

The Bernstein CP versus Skillful Opponent,   1958

WHITE: *Bernstein CP*   BLACK: *Human opponent*

1 P–K4	P–K4	4 B–KN5	B–N2
2 B–B4	P–QN3	5 B × N	Q × B
3 P–Q3	N–KB3		

"Black is preparing for a direct attack on the center, via P–Q4."

| 6 N–KB3 | P–B3 | 8 P × P | P × P |
| 7 O–O | P–Q4 | 9 B–N5+ | N–B3 |

(See Fig. II-10.)

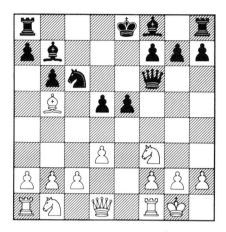

Fig. II-10.   *Position after 9 . . . , N–B3.*

10 P–B4   . . .

"White 10 N × P is better because if Black replies 10 . . . , Q × N, then 11 R–K1. Since the Pawn is defended by the Queen, 10 N × P seemingly loses material, and the move is discarded."

10 . . .   P × P   12 P × P   . . .
11 B × N+   Q × B

"White 12 is bad, R—K1 is better." (See Fig. II–11.)

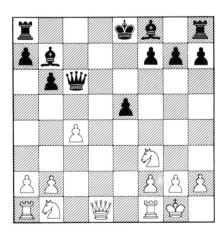

Fig. II-11.   *Position after 12 . . . , P–K5.*

12 . . .	P–K5	15 P–B3	B–B4
13 N–N5	Q–N3	16 R–K1	O–O
14 N–KR3	P–K6	17 N–B3	. . .

"Fiddling while Rome burns."

17 . . .	P–K7+	21 P–N3	R(R1)–Q1
18 N–B2	B × P	22 P–KR4	R × N
19 P–KN3	P × Q = Q	23 Resigns	
20 N(B3) × Q	Q–B7		

The Work of Newell, Shaw, and Simon (1958) *

Alan Newell, John Shaw, and Herbert Simon began work on their program in 1955 at Carnegie-Mellon University in Pittsburgh. One game played by their program is reported in [16a] and *The New York Times* reported on November 27, 1966, that a Carnegie-Mellon program lost a game to the Kotok-McCarthy program (see next chapter) in a contest played by mail over a period of several months [17].

The Newell, Shaw, and Simon (NSS) program is different than its predecessors in three respects.

(1) It is the first program written in a high-level language. The authors were involved in several artificial intelligence problems, particularly theorem proving, and were developing programming languages to use on these problems. They call their languages information processing languages (IPL's). Their chess program is coded in IPL-IV, a language designed to operate on lists and on the types of data structures that arise in chess programs.

(2) Their program uses a set of explicit goals to guide the tree search. There are no limits to the width and depth of search. The goals depend on the particular board position. The scoring function is composed of vector components, with each component being a measure of the degree of success in reaching one of the goals. The components are ordered, with material balance placed first. One position P_1 is considered better than another position P_2 if, for some k, the first k components of the scoring function of position P_1 are greater than the corresponding components for position P_2. In each position, an analysis is carried out to see if the value of any component of the scoring function might be significantly changed by making a move. If not, the position is considered dead; if so, moves relevant to the goal in question are generated. In this manner the

* See Newell *et al.* [16].

authors attempt to simulate the human mind's approach to selecting moves.

(3) Their program uses the alpha–beta algorithm.

An outgrowth of the NSS work is a special mating program called MATER [18]. MATER is written by George Baylor and Simon in FORTRAN. It is able to search to great depths for checkmates. MATER is presently part of the Cooper–Kozdrowicki program (see Chapters V–VII and IX). While MATER is an interesting program in its own right, the opportunity to checkmate one's opponent plays a relatively small computational part of the game of chess, and its inclusion in the Cooper–Kozdrowicki program does not seem to add measurably to the program's strength.

The Alpha–Beta Algorithm *

The alpha–beta algorithm supplements the minimax algorithm: it allows the computer to avoid generating irrelevant sequences of moves in a minimax search. More specifically, the alpha–beta algorithm tells the minimax algorithm to stop investigating successors of a given move or move sequence if and when a successor is found that is a *refutation move*. For example, suppose the two-ply tree in Fig. II–12 (the same tree as in Fig. II–3) is to be searched using the minimax algorithm along with the alpha–beta algorithm. The computer begins the minimax search by examining position P and generating moves M_1, M_2, and M_3. It then generates position M_1P and then moves M_{11}, M_{12}, and M_{13}. Next it generates and scores position $M_{11}P$, then $M_{12}P$, and then $M_{13}P$, concluding that, if it makes move M_1, its opponent will make move M_{12}. This leads to assigning a backed-up score of +7 to move M_1. The computer next generates position M_2P and then moves M_{21}, M_{22}, and M_{23}. It then generates and scores position $M_{21}P$ and then position $M_{22}P$. Upon finding that the score of position $M_{22}P$ is less than +7, the computer realizes that move M_2 is not as good as move M_1. Move M_{22} is called a *refutation* of move M_2. Move M_{23} need not be examined now. Its score is irrelevant. We say that move M_{22} causes a *cutoff* of the search at position M_2P. Similarly, move M_{31} refutes move M_3 and the computer need not examine moves M_{32} and M_{33}. Both of their scores are irrelevant. Thus the computer examines only six of the nine terminal positions in arriving at the conclusion that move M_1 is best. The reader should note that move M_1 also turned out to be the best move using the minimax algorithm unsupplemented by the alpha–beta algorithm.

The alpha–beta algorithm can be generalized to trees of any finite

* See Edwards and Hart [19], Slagle and Dixon [20], and Nilsson [21].

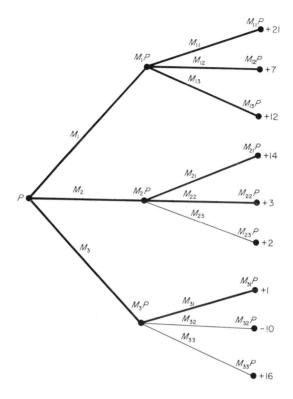

Fig. II-12. *A two-ply tree showing the alpha-beta algorithm. Branches that are examined are heavily shaded. Cutoffs occur at positions M_2P and M_3P.*

depth and even to trees of irregular depth. Cutoffs that occur at positions at odd plies are called *alpha-cutoffs*, while those that occur at positions at even plies are called *beta-cutoffs*. The four-ply tree of Fig. II-4 is shown again in Fig. II–13, but with Fig. II–13 illustrating the alpha–beta algorithm. It is assumed that terminal nodes are examined from the top to the bottom. The figure indicates by the heavy shading which branches are examined. Crosses indicate where cutoffs occur.* The reader can observe that, of the 20 terminal positions, only 8 are scored, and that it is necessary to generate successors from 11 of the 15 nonterminal nodes. The same sequence of moves found in Fig II-4, $M_1M_{11}M_{112}M_{1122}$, is again found to be the principal continuation. In general, the alpha–beta algorithm results in a great speedup of the minimax search. Under the optimal

---

* The reader might verify that M_{2111} refutes the sequence $M_2M_{21}M_{211}$, since M_1, which was examined earlier in the search, looks better than $M_2M_{21}M_{211}$.

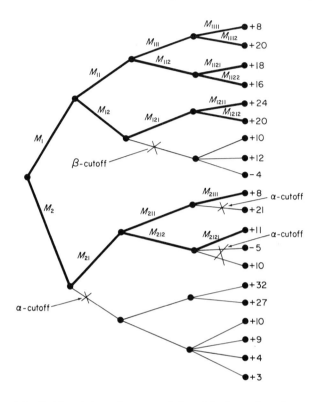

Fig. II-13. *A four-ply tree and the alpha-beta algorithm.*

case, where all possible cutoffs occur, the time to search a tree of depth d with fanout f at each node is proportional to $2f^{d/2}$; using the minimax algorithm without the alpha–beta algorithm the computation time is proportional to f^d.

The alpha–beta algorithm is an example of *backward pruning*. It finds branches from the back of the tree that are unnecessary to examine and prunes them from the tree. It is important to note that the minimax algorithm with alpha–beta and the minimax algorithm without alpha–beta yield identical principal continuations.

References

[1] Harkness, Kenneth, and Battell, Jack S., This made chess history, *Chess Review*, February–November (1947). [Column appeared monthly during this period.]
[2] Buck, Robert J., *Chess Review*, January (1947).

[3] Hagedorn, R. K., "Benjamin Franklin and Chess in Early America." Univ. of Pennsylvania Press, Philadelphia (1958).

[4] Poe, Edgar Allan, Maelzel's chess-player, *Southern Literary Messenger*, April (1836). [Also appears in Harrison, James A. (ed.), "The Complete Works of Edgar Allan Poe." Crowell, New York (1902).]

[5] Willis, Robert, An attempt to analyze the automaton chess player of Mr. De Kempelen, *Edinburgh Phil. J.* (1821).

[6] *Baltimore Gazette*, June 1, 1827.

[7] Horton, Byrne J. "Dictionary of Modern Chess." Citadel Press, New York (1972).

[8] Babbage, Charles, "The Life of a Philosopher." Longman, Green, Longman, Roberts, and Green, London (1864). [See also Morrison, P., and Morrison, E. (eds.), "Charles Babbage and His Calculating Engines." Dover, New York (1961).]

[9] Von Neumann, John, and Morgenstern, Oscar, "Theory of Games and Economic Behavior," Princeton Univ. Press, Princeton, New Jersey (1944).

[10] Wiener, Norbert, "Cybernetics." Wiley, New York (1948).

[11] Shannon, Claude, Programming a digital computer for playing chess, *Phil. Mag.* **41**, 356–375 (1950).

[12] Turing, Alan, Digital computers applied to games, *in* "Faster than Thought: A Symposium on Digital Computing Machines," Chapter 25, pp. 286–310 (B. V. Bowden, ed.). Pitman, London (1953).

[13] Kister, J., Stein, P., Ulam, S., Walden, W., and Wells, M., Experiments in chess, *JACM* **4**, 174–177 (1957).

[14] Berstein, A., Roberts, M. De V., Arbuckle, T., and Belsky, M. A., A chess playing program for the IBM 704, *Proc. Western Joint Computer Conf. 1958*, **13**, 157–159 (1958).

[15] Berstein, A., and Roberts, M. De V., Computer v. chess player, *Scientific American*, June, 96–105 (1958).

[16] Newell, A., Shaw, J., and Simon, H., Chess-playing programs and the problem of complexity, *IBM J. Res. Develop.* **2**, 320–335 (1958).

[16a] Newell, A., Shaw, J., and Simon, H., Chess-playing programs and the problem of complexity, *in* "Computers and Thought" (E. Feigenbaum and J. Feldman, eds.), pp. 39–70. McGraw-Hill, New York (1963).

[17] "Computer Chess Won by Stanford," *The New York Times*, November 27, p. 50 (1966).

[18] Baylor, G. W., and Simon, H. A., A chess mating combinations program, *Proc. Spring Joint Computer Conf., April 1966*, 431–447 (1966).

[19] Edwards, D. J., and Hart, T. P., The α–β heuristic, Artificial Intelligence Memo No. 30 (revised), MIT Research Laboratory of Electronics and Computation Center, Cambridge, Massachusetts, October 28 (1963).

[20] Slagle, J. R., and Dixon, J. K., Experiments with some programs that search game trees, *JACM* **16**, 189–207 (1969).

[21] Nilsson, Nils, "Problem Solving Methods in Artificial Intelligence." McGraw-Hill, New York (1971).

CHAPTER III

The Kotok–McCarthy Chess Program (USA) versus the ITEP Chess Program (USSR) (1966–1967)*

The inevitable happened in 1966 when a chess match was held between a program in the Soviet Union and one in the United States. The Soviet program was developed at the Institute of Theoretical and Experimental Physics (ITEP) in Moscow by George M. Adelson-Belsky, Vladimir L. Arlazarov, A. G. Ushkov, A. Bitman, and A. Zhivotovsky and used the Soviet M-20 computer during the match. The US program was the work of Alan Kotok and John McCarthy and used Stanford's IBM 7090 during the match. Play began on November 22, 1966; four games were played simultaneously with moves communicated by telegraph. The ITEP program won the match with a 3–1 victory consisting of two wins and two draws. Its first win came on March 10, 1967, when it mated the Kotok–McCarthy program in 19 moves. In one of the two games declared drawn, the ITEP program had a won position, while in the other it was ahead a Pawn and had, perhaps, a slight advantage.

At MIT and under the guidance of Professor John McCarthy, Alan Kotok developed his program as a bachelor's thesis [8]. The program is written in a combination of FORTRAN and FAP, the assembly language for the IBM 7090, and is modeled on Shannon's type-B strategy. It uses the alpha–beta algorithm along with graduated forward pruning; at deeper ply fewer successors of a position are examined. The program has the ability to search to a depth of eight ply but stops searching a move sequence whenever a "stable position" is reached. The program was tested in the spring of 1961 on an IBM 709 computer. A move took from 5 to 20

* See Refs. [1–7].

minutes. Kotok's scoring function takes into account material, center control, development, and Pawn structure. McCarthy subsequently went to Stanford, taking Kotok's program with him. Before the match, he improved the program's tree-searching algorithms.

The ITEP program was designed according to Shannon's type-A strategy. In theory, the match was intended to serve as a test of Shannon's two strategies. In actuality, the Kotok–McCarthy program was not sufficiently selective in deciding which moves could be forward pruned. As Botvinnik says, "the rule for rejecting moves was so constituted that the machine threw the baby out with the bath water" [1].

Before play started, both sides agreed that no game would exceed forty moves. The participants agreed to this condition primarily because both programs are particularly weak in end-game play. There were no restrictions made on the amount of time allowed each side to calculate its moves. The Stanford computer typically took several minutes while the ITEP computer made some moves after only several minutes of calculation and others after several hours. In Games 1 and 2, the ITEP program used a basic depth of search of three ply, while in Games 3 and 4, the basic depth of search was five ply. The Kotok–McCarthy program searched the same-sized tree in all four games. It is interesting to note that the ITEP program was only able to obtain two draws with the three-ply search, while when searching to a depth of five ply, it won both games.

In addition to playing better tactical chess, the ITEP program also played better positional chess. In particular, the ITEP programs used its Pawns more effectively. Of a total of 136 moves, the Kotok–McCarthy program made only 25 Pawn moves. Of these, only 8 were noncapturing moves by the Rooks', Knights', or Bishops' Pawns. Essentially, Pawns were never used to gain control of area or to chase away invaders. The ITEP program used its Pawns much better in this respect. Both programs made the classically weak computer-identifiable moves:

1) King and Rook moves when there is nothing better from a tactical point of view: for Kotok–McCarthy, moves 14 and 15 of Game 1 and moves 29–31 of Game 2, while for ITEP, move 28 of Game 1 and move 19 of Game 2;

(2) moves to the side of the board (some programs tend to move pieces to the side of the board): for Kotok–McCarthy, moves 31 and 33 of Game 1 and moves 12 and 17 of Game 2, and for ITEP, move 27 of Game 3;

(3) moves of pieces to squares where they can be immediately chased by a Pawn advance, thereby wasting a tempo: for Kotok–McCarthy, moves 4, 18, and 20 of Game 2, moves 8, 11, and 12 of Game 3,

and move 4 of Game 4, and for ITEP, move 6 of Game 2 and move 3 of Game 4.

Game 1   November 23, 1966

WHITE: *ITEP CP*   BLACK: *Kotok–McCarthy CP*

Four Knights Game

1 P–K4	P–K4	5 O–O	O–O
2 N–QB3	N–QB3	6 P–Q3	P–Q3
3 N–B3	B–B4	7 B–K3	B–KN5
4 B–B4	N–B3	8 P–KR3	B–R4

The ITEP CP is quick to use its Pawns to chase away invaders. (See Fig. III–1.)

9 B–Q5	B–Q5	12 B–N5	R–K1
10 P–KN4	B × N	13 R–N1	R–N1
11 P(N2) × B	B–N3	14 Q–K2	. . .

This is a tough position for a computer. White's move should be based on a long-range plan since there are no immediate tactical possibilities. But White, of course, has no such plan.

14 . . .   K–R1

White's lack of ideas is matched by a similar lack by Black!

15 P–Q4	K–N1	17 B × N	. . .
16 Q–B4	N–QR4		

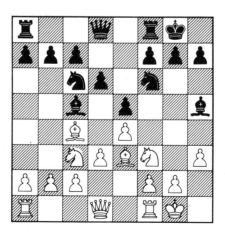

Fig. III-1.   *Position after 8 . . . , B–R4.*

White decides to simplify the position. It also delays making the necessary Queen move.

17 . . .	Q × B	19 P × P	. . .
18 Q–Q3	P–B3		

White realizes that this is necessary in order to hold its King's Pawn.

19 . . .	P × P	22 R(B1)–Q1	R–Q3
20 B–N3	R(N1)–Q1	23 P–N5	Q–K2
21 Q–K3	P–N3	24 R–Q3	R × R

Black's capture allows White to improve its Pawn structure. Black might better try 24 . . . , N–N2 threatening 25 . . . , N–B4.

25 P × R	R–Q1	26 R–R1	. . .

White looks like a computer!

26 . . .	Q–Q3	28 P × P	N × B
27 P–Q4	P × P	29 P × N	P–QR4

(See Fig. III-2.) The lack of strategy by Black becomes apparent now when it fails to realize that it must advance its Queen-side Pawns. This is Black's last Pawn move.

30 R–R4	Q–K3	32 P–B4	R–Q3
31 N–K5	Q–K1	33 P–B5	B–R4

Black exhibits the tendency to be willing to move its pieces to the side

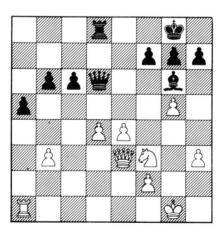

Fig. III-2. *Position after 29 . . . , P–QR4.*

of the board. Although 33 . . . , B–R4 is forced and is not a particularly bad move, Black's 31 . . . , Q–K1 was not necessary nor very good.

34 N–B4	R–Q1	37 R–R3	B–B7
35 N × P(N6)	R–N1	38 Drawn	
36 N–B4	B–Q8		

White is ahead one Pawn and may have a slight advantage. In the present position it can play 38 N–Q2. (See Fig. III-3.)

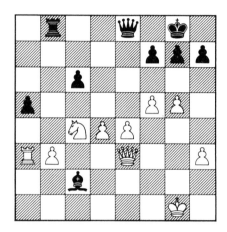

Fig. III-3. *Position at the end of the game.*

Game 2   November 23, 1966

WHITE: *Kotok–McCarthy CP*   BLACK: *ITEP CP*

Alekhine's Defense

1 P–K4	N–KB3	4 B–N5	P–QR3
2 P–K5	N–Q4	5 B–R4	P–QN4
3 N–KB3	P–K3		

The ITEP CP exhibits the same hostility toward invaders as it did in Game 1 (moves 8, 10).

| 6 B–N3 | B–N5 | 7 N–B3 | . . . |

The Kotok–McCarthy CP has no such hostility!

| 7 . . . | N–B5 | 8 O–O | B–N2 |

This is an unusual move for a computer. The fianchetto of a Bishop is rare

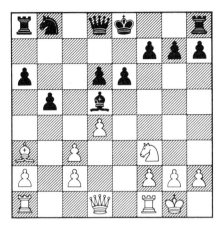

Fig. III-4. *Position after 13 . . . , P × P.*

in computer chess games except for programs selecting moves from a book.

```
 9 P–Q4      B ×N (QB3)      11 B × N     B × B
10 P × B     N–Q4           12 B–R3      . . .
```

Again, computers seem to like to move pieces to the side of the board. This moves prevents Black from castling, which is probably given credit in the Kotok–McCarthy CP.

```
12 . . .     P–Q3           13 P × P     P × P
```

(See Fig. III-4.)

```
14 R–K1      N–B3           17 Q–K1      Q–B2
15 R–K3      O–O            18 B–N4      . . .
16 Q–K2      B–B5
```

White wastes a move.

```
18 . . .     P–QR4          19 B–R3      K–R1
```

The ITEP CP is out of ideas.

```
20 N–N5      P–R3
```

Again White's invader is chased away.

```
21 N–K4      R(B1)–Q1       24 P–QR3     N–K2
22 N X P     R × N          25 R–K5      N–B3
23 B × R     Q × B
```

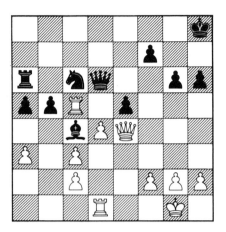

Fig. III-5. *Position after 28 . . . , P–N3.*

The invaders never seem to get discouraged.

26 R–QB5   P–K4   27 Q–K4   R–R3

This move is characteristic of computer chess moves: Rooks often move forward one or two squares. Much better from a positional point of view is 27 . . . , R–QB1.

28 R–Q1   P–N3

(See Fig. III-5.) This move, consistent with the ITEP CP's style, prevents White from playing 29 Q–B5 or 29 Q–N4 followed by 30 Q–B8.

29 R–Q2   P–N4   30 R–Q1   P–R5

Both sides are somewhat out of ideas. Black, however, must give more credit for advancing Pawns than does White.

31 R–Q2	P–B3	36 R–B8+	K–R2
32 Q–K3	P × P	37 R–B8	P–QN5
33 P × P	N–K2	38 P × P	N × P
34 Q–KN3	Q × Q	39 P–QB3	N–Q4
35 P(R2) × Q	N–Q4	40 R–B8	Drawn

Black should be able to force White to give up material in order to pre-vent the Rook's Pawn from queening.

Game 3   November 23, 1966*

WHITE: *ITEP CP*   BLACK: *Kotok–McCarthy CP*

Three Knights Game

1 P–K4	P–K4	3 N–B3	B–B4
2 N–KB3	N–QB3	4 N × P	N × N

Botvinnik suggests that "4 . . . , B × P+, 5 K × B, N × N, 6 P–Q4 was better" for Black. White's 4 N × P requires a 6-ply search to see that material is not lost. In the same position in Game 1, White, while looking only 3 ply deep, chose 4 B–B4 instead of the somewhat more adventurous 4 N × P. In performing an exhaustive 5-ply search, the ITEP program must investigate capturing sequences beyond this limit.

5 P–Q4	B–Q3	7 P–B4	B × N+
6 P × N	B × P	8 P × B	N–B3

(See Fig. III-6.) Black invites trouble. An adequate move for Black was 8 . . . , P–Q3. Black will make 5 consecutive Knight moves and finally lose both it and the game.

9 P–K5	N–K5	10 Q–Q3	N–B4

Black might have tried 10 . . . , P–Q4. If 11 P × P e.p., then 11 . . . , N × P(Q3).

11 Q–Q5   N–K3

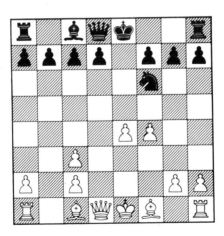

Fig. III-6.   *Position after 8 . . . , N–B3.*

* Botvinnik presents an analysis of this game in his book [1].

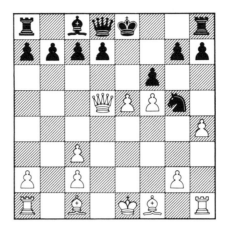

Fig. III-7. *Position after 13 . . . , P–KB3.*

Botvinnik indicates that Black must play 11 . . . , P–Q3. Black's position is getting more precarious with every Knight move.

12 P–B5   N–N4   13 P–KR4   P–KB3

(See Fig. III-7.) Black cannot see far enough ahead to realize that this move will get it into serious trouble. It is simply concerned with not losing too much material and feels that 13 . . . , P–KB3, 14 P×N, P×P will minimize the loss. It does not see the real danger just over the horizon in White's move 15 R×P!

14 P × N	P × P(N4)	17 Q–Q6	R × P
15 R × P	R–B1	18 R–N8+	R–B1
16 R × P	P–B3	19 Q × R mate	

Game 4   November 23, 1966

WHITE: *Kotok–McCarthy CP*   BLACK: *ITEP CP*

Alekhine's Defense

1 P–K4   N–KB3   3 N–KB3   N–N5
2 P–K5   N–Q4   4 B–N5   . . .

While ignoring the opportunity to chase away Black's Knight, the Kotok–McCarthy CP exposes its own Bishop to an imminent attack. We should expect the ITEP program to chase away the Bishop immediately.

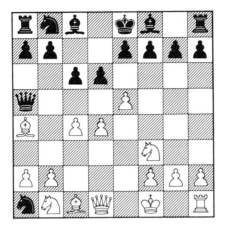

Fig. III-8. *Position after* 8 . . . , N × R.

4 . . .	P–QB3	6 P–Q4	Q–R4
5 B–R4	P–Q3	7 P–B4	. . .

A serious blunder is made by White. White's moves 7, 12, and 18 are unusually weak and reflect shortcomings in the forward-pruning algorithms or possibly simply a programming bug.

7 . . .	N–B7++	8 K–B1	N × R

(See Fig. III-8.) Any good human playing White would attempt to recover at least some of his loss by making sure that the trapped Knight is eventually recaptured. A computer however has a very poor attention span. It cannot immediately recapture the Knight and does not realize that it is, in fact, trapped and cannot get away. Thus watch how White allows its opportunity to recapture the trapped Knight to evaporate.

9 N–B3	Q–N5	11 P × P	B–K3
10 Q–K2	P × P		

Black threatens to pin the Queen.

12 Q–Q1	. . .

This is White's second very bad move. White overlooked 12 N–Q2, which might have slowed down the disaster.

12 . . .	B × P+	14 B–B2	N × B
13 N–K2	P–QN4	15 Q × N	. . .

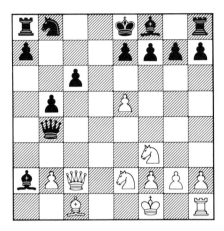

Fig. III-9. *Position after 15 . . . , B × P.*

White has lost its chance to recapture the Knight. Black can hardly miss winning now.

15 . . .   B × P

(See Fig. III-9.) One might argue that Black should have made a developing move rather than win the remote Rook's Pawn. Computers, however, do not reason this way. The Pawn capture outweighs any positional gain that a developing move might provide.

16 N(K2)–Q4   Q–B5+   18 Q–Q2   . . .
17 K–N1   P–QB4

The third serious error is made.

18 . . .   P × N   20 N–B3   N–B3
19 N × P   P–K3   21 Q–N5   . . .

White's move is another example of the style of chess played by computers. The Queen is prone to wandering off to remote corners of the board.

21 . . .   R–Q1

Black threatens mate with 22 . . . , R–Q8.

22 B–Q2   Q–B8+   24 Q–B4   B–Q4
23 B–K1   Q × P

A sure-fire long-range strategy for Black at this point might be to advance its Queen-side Pawns while trading pieces, eventually queening a Pawn or forcing a further material loss by White. Black instead searches for a tactical win and is helped by White's weak play.

25	Q–N3	Q–K7	29	K–N2	Q × P(K4)
26	B–B3	P–N5	30	Q–R4	P–QR4
27	B–K1	B × N	31	R–QB1	N–Q5
28	P × B	Q × B+	32	R–B1	N × P

Black must have seen that if 33 K × N, then 33 . . . , R–Q5 followed by 34 Q × R, Q × Q or 34 Q–R3, R–Q6+ gives it a still larger advantage.

33	Q–R3	R–Q6	38	K–K1	R–R8+
34	Q–N3	N–K8+	39	K–Q2	Q–Q4+
35	R × N	R × Q+	40	K–K3	R–R6+
36	K–B1	Q–N4+	41	K–B4	Q–KB4 mate
37	R–K2	R–QR6			

References

[1] Botvinnik, M. M., "Computers, Chess, and Long Range Planning" pp. 1–5 (English trans.). Springer-Verlag, Berlin and New York (1970).

[2] "U.S. Computer Battling Soviets' in Chess Game," *The New York Times,* November 22, p. 3 (1966).

[3] Anderson, R. H., Electronic chess is won by soviet, *The New York Times,* November 26, p. 146 (1967).

[4] "Soviet Computer's Chess Win," *The Times (London),* November 21, p. 5 (1967).

[5] *Chess,* April, 251–252 (1968). [Comments on the match following a Levy/Good article that appeared on pp. 242–250.]

[6] " Шахматный Матч Машин ," *Izvestiia,* November 23, p. 4 (1966).

[7] *SIGART Newsletter, ACM* (4), 11, June (1967). [Presents progress in Kotok–McCarthy vs. ITEP match.]

[8] Kotok, Allen, "A Chess Playing Program for IBM 7090," B.S. Thesis, MIT, Cambridge, Massachusetts (1962).

[9] Adelson-Belsky, G. M., Arlazaroff, V. L., Bitman, A. R., Zhivotovsky, A. A., and Uskov, A. V., Programming a computer to play chess, *Russian Math. Surveys* **25,** 221–262, March–April, 1970.

CHAPTER IV

The Greenblatt Chess Program (1967)

Richard Greenblatt was an undergraduate at MIT when he began work on his chess program. He was assisted by Donald Eastlake and Stephen Crocker. The work was performed at MIT's Artificial Intelligence Laboratory and was supported by Project MAC. Work began in November 1966, and the state of the program as of August 1967 was presented at the 1967 Fall Joint Computer Conference [1].

Greenblatt's program, named Mac Hack Six, represents a landmark in the history of chess programs—being the first to compete respectably against humans in tournament play. It played in several tournaments in the Boston area in the spring of 1967 and earned a rating of about 1400, a level comparable with that of a good high school player. Greenblatt reports that his program had played several hundred games.

Mac Hack Six was written for the PDP-6. Greenblatt wrote the program in MIDAS, the assembly language for the PDP-6. He reports that the program requires 16K words of memory. A version of Mac Hack Six is presently available on many time-sharing services that use Digital Equipment Corporation's PDP series computers. Most chess programs developed in the United States in the last few years have competed informally against Mac Hack Six via this service [4–9]. The program is also available on the ARPA network.

Mac Hack Six is designed along Shannon's type-B strategy. Forward pruning is used extensively along with the alpha–beta algorithm. At tournament settings, Mac Hack Six searches a tree of moves having a minimum fanout of 15 moves at ply 1, 15 at ply 2, 9 at ply 3, 9 at ply 4, and 7 at deeper plies. However, at each node the minimum number may be exceeded to ensure that:

(1) All safe checks are investigated (a safe check is a legal checking move that does not leave the checking piece en prise);

(2) All captures at ply 1 and 2 are investigated; and

(3) Moves by some minimum number of different pieces are considered.

Moves that lead to mate in one by the opponent are not included in the count and thus, if there is a way to avoid mate in one, Mac Hack Six will find it.

Mac Hack Six speeds up the tree search by storing in a table each position as it is assigned a score along with its score. If the same position is reached later in the search through a permutation of moves, it is considered a terminal position and its score is found in the table. Time is saved by not having to search successors of this position.

At tournament settings, Mac Hack Six searches to a depth of four ply and extends the search one ply at a time to a depth of six ply if certain conditions exist on the board at the fourth or deeper plies:

(1) The side to move has a piece en prise and (a) is in check or (b) the en prise piece is trapped or pinned;

(2) The side to move has two or more pieces en prise;

(3) Both sides have one piece en prise with the piece of the side not to move trapped or pinned while the opponent's piece is not trapped or pinned.

When a terminal position is evaluated, the static board evaluator develops a score for the position using five factors. An exploration of all sequences of favorable captures from that position is also performed with no depth limit to allow for a more accurate material evaluation. The five factors of the scoring function are: (1) material, (2) material ratio, (3) Pawn structure, (4) King safety, and (5) center control. The material ratio factor encourages Mac Hack Six to trade pieces when ahead and not to trade when behind. Pawn structure takes into account tripled Pawns, doubled isolated Pawns, isolated Pawns, and passed Pawns. King safety encourages the King to remain on the back rank when Queens are on the board; this factor does not apply when the Queens are missing. Center control encourages Pawns to occupy the middle squares.

Greenblatt states that his program uses about 50 heuristics in establishing the plausibility of a given move. These excellent heuristics, along with its being quite well debugged, permit Mack Hack Six to play at a level far above its predecessors. We present here two of its games. The first game is Mac Hack Six's first tournament victory. Its opponent had a 1510 USCF rating. Mac Hack Six ran on a PDP-6. The second game was played against a program written by J. J. Scott of the University of Lancaster, England. Scott's program ran on an ICL 1909/5 computer; Greenblatt's ran on a PDP-10. A report of Scott's work along with an analysis of this game appears in *Machine Intelligence* [2, 3].

The following game was played in Game 3, Tournament 2, of the Massachusetts State Championship in 1967.

WHITE: *Mac Hack Six*   BLACK: *Human (USCF rating: 1510)*

Sicilian Opening

1 P–K4   P–QB4   2 P–Q4   . . .

Mac Hack Six is always eager to initiate an attack. This seems to be the most characteristic feature of its play. In this game Mac Hack Six's Queen enters the battle on the third move. Black plays very timidly and never attempts to make life difficult for the Queen, soon finding himself in serious trouble.

2 . . .	P × P	7 B–B4	P–K4
3 Q × P	N–QB3	8 B–N3	P–QR3
4 Q–Q3	N–B3	9 O–O–O	P–QN4
5 N–QB3	P–KN3	10 P–QR4	B–R3+
6 N–B3	P–Q3		

Black has left his Queen's Pawn undefended. This and Black's next two moves play into Mac Hack Six's hands. Black must lose at least a couple of Pawns. Mac Hack Six makes a series of consistently strong moves, clinching the game on move 15, when it forces Black to give up his Queen for a Knight.

11 K–N1   P–N5

(See Fig. IV-1.)

12 Q × P(Q6)	B–Q2	15 N–B7+	Q × N
13 B–R4	B–N2	16 Q × Q	N–B4
14 N–Q5	N × P	17 Q–Q6	. . .

Mac Hack Six's Queen continues to keep the pressure on Black.

17 . . .	B–KB1	19 N × P	B–K3
18 Q–Q5	R–B1		

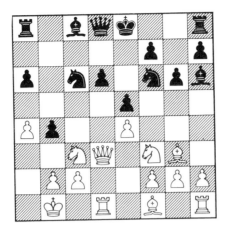

Fig. IV-1. *Position after 11 . . . , P–N5.*

Black sets up mate in two for White.

20 Q × N(B6+)   R × Q   21 R–Q8 mate

In the following game, since the Scott CP cannot castle, the first four moves were agreed upon before the computers took control. Mac Hack Six was set to average 25 sec per move while the Scott CP was set to average 90 sec per move in an effort to balance the capabilities of the two computers. (Good [3] presents an analysis of this game.)

WHITE: *Scott CP*   BLACK: *Mac Hack Six*

1 P–KN3	P–KN3	5 N–B3	N–B3
2 N–KB3	N–KB3	6 P–Q4	P–Q4
3 B–N2	B–N2	7 N–K5	Q–Q3
4 O–O	O–O	8 N × N	Q × N

Mac Hack avoids isolating the Queen's Rook's Pawn.

9 B–N5	R–Q1	11 P–QR3	. . .
10 Q–Q2	B–K3		

The Scott CP gives credit for Pawn advancement. Since there is nothing else pressing, this small credit is enough to give this move the best score.

11 . . .   P–QR4   12 Q–Q3   . . .

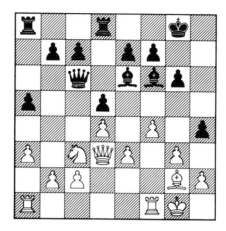

Fig. IV-2.   *Position after 15 . . . , P–KR5.*

White forgets why it moved its Queen to Q2.

| 12 . . . | P–R3 | 14 P–K3 | P–R4 |
| 13 B × N | B × B | 15 P–B4 | P–KR5 |

(See Fig. IV-2.) Mac Hack Six is attempting to isolate White's King's Rook's Pawn. This is a relatively closed position and the only factor in the scoring functions of both programs influencing the choice of moves seems to be Pawn structure.

| 16 P × P | B × P(R5) | 17 K–R1 | B–B3 |

Two moves are wasted. Black should be planning to exert pressure on the open Rook file with, for example, 17 . . . , K–N2.

| 18 Q–K2 | R–R3 | 20 N–N5 | B–B4 |
| 19 P–QR4 | R–N3 | | |

Mac Hack Six continues to attack White's pieces.

| 21 P–B3 | B–K5 | 22 B × B | P × B |

Mack Hack Six has given itself a weak Pawn on K5.

| 23 P–B4 | P–K3 | 25 N–B3 | K–N2 |
| 24 P–QB5 | R–R3 | 26 P–R3 | . . . |

White overlooked 26 Q–N2, which wins a Pawn. There are 40 legal moves in this position.

| 26 . . . | B–K2 | 27 P–N3 | . . . |

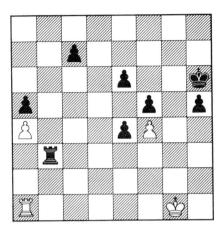

Fig. IV-3. *Position after 44 . . . , R × P.*

White's play continues to show no planning. Both sides should be attempting to force an advantage on the King's side.

27 . . .	P–B4	30 R–B1	B–K2
28 K–N2	B–B3	31 R–KR1	R–KR1
29 R(R1)–K1	B–R5	32 R–QR1	. . .

Fantastic!

| 32 . . . | B–B3 | 34 Q × Q | R × Q |
| 33 Q–N5 | R–Q1 | 35 P–R4 | P–N3 |

White's Queen-side Pawns are in serious trouble. White chooses to play an "ostrich" move!

| 36 P–R5 | P × P(R4) | 37 R(KR1)–KN1 | . . . |

For the second time, the Scott CP overlooks winning a Pawn. White will find itself two Pawns behind very shortly.

| 37 . . . | P × P | 39 N–N5 | P × P |
| 38 K–B2+ | K–R3 | 40 N × P(Q4) | R × N |

Good says that this is "slightly better than 40 . . . , B × N since it reduces the material more."

| 41 P × R | B × P+ | 43 K–N2 | B × R |
| 42 K–N3 | R–B6+ | 44 K × B | R × P |

(See Fig. IV-3.) Black is now four Pawns ahead and can hardly miss.

45 R–QB1	P–K6	52 K–B2	P–R6
46 R × P	K–N3	53 K–B3	P–R7
47 K–B1	R–N5	54 R–KR8	R–R7
48 K–K2	R × P(B5)	55 K–N3	R–K7
49 K × P	R–K5+	56 K–R4	K–N2
50 K–Q3	P–R5	57 R–R3	R–R7+
51 R–B8	R × P	58 K–N5	. . .

The use of the King is particularly weak in end-game play because he is given no eyes to see where to go!

58 . . .   P–K4   59 Resigns

References

[1] Greenblatt, R. D., Eastlake, D. E., and Crocker, S. D., The Greenblatt chess program, *Proc. Fall Joint Computer Conf., 1967*, 801–810, AFIPS Press, Montvale, New Jersey (1967).

[2] Scott, J. J., A chess playing program, *Machine Intelligence*, 255–265 (1969).

[3] Good, I. J., Analysis of Machine Chess Game, J. Scott (White), ICL–1900 vs. R. D. Greenblatt, PDP-10, *Machine Intelligence*, 267–269 (1969).

References to Other Games Played by Mac Hack Six

[4] Berliner, Hans, Experiences gained in constructing and testing a chess program, *IEEE Symp. System Sci. Cybernetics*, Pittsburgh, Pennsylvania, October, 1970.

[5] *SIGART Newsletter*, ACM (6), 8, October (1967).

[6] *SIGART Newsletter*, ACM (9), 9–10, April (1968).

[7] *SIGART Newsletter*, ACM (15), 8–10, April (1969).

[8] *SIGART Newsletter*, ACM (16), 9–11, June (1969).

[9] *SIGART Newsletter*, ACM (39), 23, April (1973).

CHAPTER V

The First United States Computer Chess Championship (New York, 1970)

Early in the spring of 1970, Kenneth M. King, who was then director of the Columbia University Computer Center, and the author became co-chairmen of the Special Events Program for the Association for Computing Machinery's (ACM) 1970 Annual Conference held from August 31 to September 2 at the Hilton Hotel in New York City. The ACM is the oldest professional organization in the United States for computer specialists. Its annual conferences are highlighted by their technical programs at which typically 100–200 papers covering all aspects of the computer field are presented. Traditionally, the ACM's Special Events Programs have served to supplement the conferences' technical programs. Their function has been to provide the conference attendees interesting computer-related activities when they are not attending the technical sessions.

While searching for ideas for the Special Events Program, we received a letter from Tony Marsland, who was then a researcher at the Bell Telephone Laboratories. Marsland wondered whether we were interested in using a computer chess program that he had developed. He suggested a demonstration at the conference; his program would either play another program or pit itself against human competition. This suggested other exciting possibilities. We felt that the time was ripe to gather all computer programs in existence in the United States and find out which one was actually best. We hoped this would also stimulate interest in the field of artificial intelligence by providing a focal point for individuals to meet and discuss their ideas. With Marsland's help, the five other teams that participated were contacted.

Marsland's interest in computer chess began in the late 1960s when he was a doctoral student at the University of Washington, in Seattle. His work was carried out under Professor Dan Johnson. At the same time Ed Kozdrowicki, also a student of Johnson's, developed an interest in chess programming. Kozdrowicki subsequently joined the faculty of the Department of Electrical Engineering at the University of California, Davis, where he collaborated with a student, Dennis Cooper, on a full-fledged chess program. Cooper (now at the Bell Telephone Laboratories, Whippany, New Jersey) and Kozdrowicki have continued to work together on their program despite the inconvenience of being 3000 miles apart. Thus, when the search for programs began, Cooper was contacted; he was quite excited about having their program COKO III participate in the tournament.

About this time computer trade journals were publishing stories about a minicomputer that played chess. The computer turned out to be an IDIOM system, developed by a small company in the New York area, Information Displays, Inc. The IDIOM system had an elaborate graphical display of the chess board; moves were made on the display by using a light pen—one simply pointed to the square of the piece to be moved and the square to which the piece was to be moved. This information was then transmitted to the main computer, a Varian 620/i. The Varian 620/i is a minicomputer having only 4K of memory. We contacted the president, Kenneth L. King,* and he agreed to bring the system to the Hilton and to compete against the other giant systems. The program for the IDIOM was written by Chris Daly, a researcher at the NASA, Goddard Space Flight Center, Goddard, Maryland.

Marsland steered us to (1) the Northwestern University group of Larry Atkin, Keith Gorlen, and David Slate and their program, CHESS 3.0, (2) the Texas A & M team of Franklin Ceruti and Rolf Smith and their program, SCHACH, and (3) Hans Berliner of Carnegie-Mellon University and his program, J. Biit. We also encouraged Richard Greenblatt to enter Mac Hack Six. He declined, however, implying that Mac Hack Six was developed as part of an artificial intelligence project whose purpose was to model the human thought process, and that to have it compete against other computers would, in some sense, be contrary to its objectives. Greenblatt has been invited to enter Mac Hack Six in each of the four ACM tournaments and he has declined each time. It is not clear at all whether the 1968 version of his program would have won the tournament. The author feels that it would have been a very close match between Mac Hack Six and CHESS 3.0. More recent versions of Atkin,

---

* There are two Kenneth Kings.

Gorlen, and Slate's program seem to be better than Greenblatt's. In fact, several of the programs in the 1972 and 1973 tournaments seem at least as good as Mac Hack Six. Greenblatt has reportedly made improvements in Mack Hack Six since 1968, but there has been no published material reporting them.

Hans Berliner, a doctoral student working under Professor Allen Newell in the Department of Computer Science at Carnegie-Mellon, needed a computer in order for his program to participate in the tournament. It was not possible for his program to use the computer on the Carnegie-Mellon campus during the tournament. His program was written in PL1 for the IBM 360/65 at Carnegie-Mellon and was supposed to be compatible with other large IBM 360 series machines. Ken King felt it would be exciting if Berliner were to use Columbia's powerful IBM 360/91; so an invitation was extended to Berliner and he accepted. When he came to New York two weeks before the tournament to modify his program for the IBM 360/91 he found there were many programming changes necessary and he frantically worked to finish them on time. He was assisted by several systems programmers at Columbia, most notably Steve Bellovin, Aron Eisenpress, Andrew Koenig, and Benjamin Yalow. After the tournament was over, the Columbia systems programmers met and decided that, while they enjoyed helping Berliner, the following year they would have a program of their own—they did, but it was not at the level of Berliner's.

The rules that governed play were formulated several weeks before the tournament. Meeting to decide on the rules were Keith Gorlen, Dennis Cooper, Tony Marsland, and the author. The rules were relatively easy to agree upon with the exception of one. We all agreed that each computer should be required to make all its moves within some arbitrary time allotment, but Marsland felt that the allotment given to each computer should depend on the speed of the computer; faster computers should receive less time than slower ones. The rest of us felt that it would be impossible to handicap the computers fairly; there were other factors besides speed that made one computer "better" than another. Thus, while it certainly was not the ideal solution for all involved, it was decided that all computers should receive equal amounts of time to make their moves. A rate of 40 moves in the first two hours and 10 moves every subsequent half hour was agreed upon. The rules also included time-out provisions in the case of system failures, communication failures, etc. These time-outs were frequently used in the 1970 and somewhat less in the 1971, 1972, and 1973 tournaments.

Jacques Dutka, a mathematician and former Master, served as tournament director. He is best known for his calculation of $\sqrt{2}$ to 1,000,000 decimal digits accuracy! This was accomplished on the Columbia University IBM 360/91 computer several months after the completion of the 1970 tournament.

The Tournament *

The three-round Swiss-system** tournament was held in the Rhinelander Room in the New York Hilton Hotel on the evenings of August 31 to September 2. Computers were connected to the Rhinelander Room via telephones from Illinois, Texas, New Jersey, and two New York City locations; the IDIOM system was at the site of the tournament. At 5:30 each evening the games were scheduled to begin, but more typically they began around 6 P.M. It was a rare event throughout the tournament when all three games were simultaneously in progress. Almost always at least one computer was having difficulties. However, in general, the better programs were more reliable, and in turn the better games usually had fewer interruptions. Each evening there were several hundred spectators in attendance, including computer specialists and chess experts. The most notable chess experts were Pal Benko, one of the top players in the United States, who seemed somewhat unsure of the future potential of computers in the chess world, and Al Horowitz, former chess editor of the New York Times, a long-time skeptic regarding their potential.

Throughout the tournament there was a most casual and informal atmosphere in the Rhinelander Room. Good moves were met with cheers from the audience; bad moves were hissed. The programmers discussed moves they expected their computers to make, reporters interviewed the participants, and Berliner ate his sandwiches. Berliner, an old pro of the human chess tournament circuit, came well stocked with food each evening.

The tournament began with considerable speculation regarding who was best. The author felt that the contenders were J. Biit, the Marsland CP, COKO III, and CHESS 3.0, with a slight edge to J. Biit.

The first round saw J. Biit clinch a fast victory over Marsland's program. The Marsland CP apparently had at least one serious programming bug, which is discussed in the annotations of the game. J. Biit played well and, with the exception of a weak sixth move, its ten-move victory supported our early speculation. Meanwhile, on Board 2, COKO

---

* See references [1–5].

** In a Swiss-system tournament, no team is eliminated. Before the tournament begins the tournament director orders the teams according to their anticipated strength. Then in round 1, team 1 plays team 4, team 2 plays team 5, and team 3 plays team 6 (assuming 6 teams). As the tournament proceeds, an attempt is made in each round to pair teams with identical scores.

III tangled with CHESS 3.0 and, with J. Biit's game over so quickly and the game on Board 3 having many computer system problems, this game became the center of attention. The game was an exciting battle for 33 moves. Then on move 34, COKO III allowed CHESS 3.0 to advance a Pawn to the sixth rank. The Pawn queened on move 42, assisted by a COKO III blunder on move 41. COKO III resigned on move 44. CHESS 3.0 had won its first game; it simply gave up no material, pushed a Pawn, and then, while in a winning position, had the game handed to it. Although a clear victory, it did not convince the supporters of Berliner's program that CHESS 3.0 was the better program. The third board turned out to be somewhat of a surprise victory for the Daly CP and the IDIOM minicomputer. The Daly CP simply harassed SCHACH with its aggressive Queen. Neither side developed to any degree. Additionally, SCHACH had two serious problems that helped lead to its downfall. It had a serious programming bug that accounted for a terrible 6th move, and for unexplained reasons its system frequently crashed throughout the game.

On the second evening CHESS 3.0 and and J. Biit met. By move 6, CHESS 3.0 had isolated J. Biit's Queen's Rook's Pawn. It won a Pawn on move 13, traded a Bishop and a Pawn for a Rook on moves 19–21, and then gradually increased its advantage while pushing its King's Pawn to the eighth rank, finally mating J. Biit on move 50. CHESS 3.0 had clearly established its superiority over the other programs by the end of this evening. In the other two games, COKO III resoundingly defeated the Daly CP and SCHACH gained a victory over the problem-plagued Marsland CP.

CHESS 3.0 met SCHACH on the third evening. Going into the final evening SCHACH, J. Biit, COKO III, and the Daly CP all had earned one point and were tied for second place. CHESS 3.0, with two points, needed merely a draw to win the championship. It had no serious problem defeating SCHACH in 31 moves, although SCHACH had an opportunity to make things difficult for CHESS 3.0 on move 13. COKO III and J. Biit meanwhile played an 87-move game that ended in a draw. Both sides had opportunities to win. The game ended with each side having two Pawns and a King. The two Kings wandered aimlessly around, and eventually a position was repeated for the third time. Well before the end of this game, the Daly CP defeated the Marsland CP, and the audience and players were thus waiting to see whether J. Biit or COKO III would tie the Daly CP for second place. This did not happen. The Daly CP gained second place by being the only team with two victories. Both victories could be primarily attributed to the reliability of the IDIOM system in contrast to the erratic behavior of the systems that it defeated.

Thus CHESS 3.0 walked off with the first place title, much to the satisfaction of Atkin, Gorlen, and Slate. No less enthusiastic was Ben Mittman, director of the Vogelback Computer Center. Mittman shortly thereafter agreed to organize the second tournament for the following year at the ACM's 1971 Conference in Chicago.

Brief Description of Programs [*]

Chess 3.0

An outstanding narrative of the history of the Northwestern chess program is given in the science fiction magazine *Analog* [6]. The three authors of CHESS 3.0, Larry Atkin, Keith Gorlen, and David Slate, were students at Northwestern when their project began. In early 1968, Atkin and Gorlen, both undergraduates, developed a very weak chess program. Shortly thereafter, Slate, a graduate student in physics and an excellent

TABLE V-1

Final Standings of the First United States Computer Chess Championship

Program, authors, computer, location of computer	Round 1	Round 2	Round 3	Points
1. CHESS 3.0 Larry Atkin, Keith Gorlen, David Slate CDC 6400, Northwestern Univ.	W4	W3	W5	3
2. The Daly CP Chris Daly, Kenneth L. King IDIOM System with a Varian 620/i, located at site of tournament	W5	L4	W6	2
3. J. Biit Hans Berliner IBM 360/91, Columbia Univ.	W6	L1	D4	1½
4. COKO III Dennis Cooper, Ed Kozdrowicki IBM 360/65, Bell Telephone Laboratories Whippany, N. J.	L1	W2	D3	1½
5. SCHACH Franklin Ceruti, Rolf Smith IBM 360/65, Texas A&M Univ.	L2	W6	L1	1
6. The Marsland CP Tony Marsland Burroughs B5500, Burrough's Sales Office, New York City, N.Y.	L3	L5	L2	0

[*] See Table V-1.

chess player, heard about their work and decided to write a program of his own. Sometime late in 1968 or early 1969 the three joined forces, realizing they could make faster progress by combining Slate's chess strength and Atkin's and Gorlen's strength in the area of computer software. In October 1969 their first completed joint effort emerged—CHESS 2.0. Between then and the time of the First United States Computer Chess Championship, they made improvements in its tree-searching heuristics and evaluation function, increased its speed by 65%, and called it CHESS 3.0.

CHESS 3.0 runs on the CDC 6000 and 7000 series computers. It is written in COMPASS, the assembly language for the CDC 6000 and 7000 series computers, and consists of about 6000 60-bit words. The authors state that CHESS 3.0 typically examines about 10,000 board positions when selecting a move that requires 3 minutes of computation. The program uses the alpha–beta algorithm. A book subroutine selects the first few moves in each game. While no detailed description of CHESS 3.0 has been published, its successor CHESS 3.5 is described in two articles [7, 8].

J. Biit

Hans Berliner began work on his program, which he named J. Biit (Just Because It Is There), in May 1968. Berliner was motivated by the work of Greenblatt, and his approach reflects the sophistication of an outstanding chess player. A good description of his program can be found in Berliner [9]. Most notably, his program searches a very small tree, carrying out considerable analysis at each node. He claims that on the average only 30 nodes in the tree are examined for a move that requires 65 sec of calculation!

Work on J. Biit started when Berliner was an employee of IBM and continued when he became a graduate student at Carnegie-Mellon University. J. Biit is written in PL/1, version IV. It used about 200,000 bytes of 8-bit words of memory when it ran on the Columbia University IBM 360/91 during the tournament. The program itself contains slightly in excess of 3500 PL/1 statements.

J. Biit uses the alpha–beta algorithm. In addition, Berliner developed a "free form of search which terminated in quiescent positions . . . (with) the only bound being the absolute depth limit of 14 ply." Normally, search is carried out to a minimum of two ply in early and middle-game positions and four ply in end-game positions. J. Biit uses incremental updating of board positions, and Berliner indicates in his paper that the introduction of this technique "speeded up the program by a factor of four"!

J. Biit contains a book with "approximately 200 selected lines of play." Berliner notes that the lines must be selected very carefully and fitted to the program's ability and style of play. If a book opening is "unnatural" for the program's style of play, the program will often waste moves when leaving book, attempting to return to a more natural position. Also when leaving book early because of a move by its opponent, a program does not hypothesize that there might exist a strong reply; it does not hypothesize that the opponent might have made a weak move. It simply plays on in its usual blind fashion. Chess programs could be written to do this, but to date this has not been done.

Berliner's paper presents a game that J. Biit played against Mac Hack Six. The game ended in a draw by repetition on move 28. Berliner's paper concludes by stating that he feels Greenblatt's 1968 version of Mac Hack is somewhat stronger that J. Biit. He also states that he expects to stop work on J. Biit and apply the knowledge gained to date to write a stronger program.

Coko III *

As stated earlier, COKO III was developed by Dennis Cooper and Ed Kozdrowicki. The most relevant features of COKO III are (1) a sophisticated tree-searching algorithm [10], (2) MATER, the mating program of Baylor and Simon [12], and (3) its machine independence; COKO III was written in FORTRAN IV and has been executed on the IBM 7044, the IBM 360/50, 65, and 91, the PDP 10, the UNIVAC 1108, and the B5500/6500. COKO III is a very tactically oriented program—it searches for pins, checks, forks, etc., very explicitly with a set of subroutines, each of which has a specific tactical objective.

COKO III's most serious shortcoming is that it automatically stops searching its tree when the time limit for a move has been reached. Typically only 4–8 moves at the first level of the tree might be examined. A second shortcoming is its stress on tactical play; a move with tactical potentials is almost always selected over a move with positional value.

Because of its emphasis on tactical play, when COKO III is in an end-game position it moves very quickly, since there are very few tactical considerations. Its play consequently weakens.

Schach **

Rolf Smith and Franklin Ceruti developed their program while they were graduate students at Texas A&M. Their effort began in 1968. SCHACH is written in FORTRAN IV and has been executed on many

* See Kozdrowicki [10, 11].
** See Refs. [7], [8], and [14].

different computers. It required a relatively large amount of memory space: 72K with overlays, 135K without. SCHACH searches a fairly small tree in arriving at a move, and that, along with a number of programming bugs, prevented it from performing as well as the better programs. Its best game was its loss to CHESS 3.0 in the third round.

The Marsland Chess Program

The Marsland CP was developed when Marsland was a graduate student at the University of Washington. Being a computer scientist and originally coming from England, he wrote the program appropriately enough in Extend ALGOL for the Burroughs B5500/B6500 computers.

The Daly Chess Program

Daly developed his program explicitly for the IDIOM system and wrote it in the assembly language for the Varian 620/i, the central processing unit of the IDIOM. The program requires only 4K of memory. It uses the alpha–beta algorithm, searches all moves out to a depth of 4 ply, and uses only material and mobility as factors to determine what move to make. Daly essentially implemented Shannon's type-A strategy, using a slightly different scoring function.

Date: 8/31/70   Round: 1   Board: 1 *

WHITE: *The Marsland CP*   BLACK: *J. Biit*

On September 2, 1972, *The New York Times* published a story covering the first evening of the 1970 tournament. The headline was, "Chess Computer Loses Game in King-Size Blunder"; the reporter was John Devlin. Devlin's article includes a listing of this game and a few comments by Al Horowitz, former chess editor of *The New York Times* and an International Grandmaster.

| 1 P–QB4 | N–KB3 | 3 Q–Q3 | . . . |
| 2 P–Q4 | P–K3 | | |

The Queen develops too early.

| 3 . . . | N–B3 | 5 N–K5 | P × P |
| 4 N–KB3 | P–Q4 | 6 Q × P(B4) | . . . |

* Note: Neither side recorded the times of its moves. At the end of the game White's clock indicated that 26 minutes were used, Black's indicated 12 minutes.

This move loses a Pawn through 6 . . . , Q × P.

6 . . .   B–N5+   8 K × B   . . .
7 B–Q2   B × B+

White selects the worst move. Most likely a programming bug caused the tree-searching algorithm to confuse good scores with bad scores.

8 . . .   N × N   9 Q–B5   . . .

Again the worst move is selected.

9 . . .   N–K5+   10 Resigns

(See Fig. V-1.)

Date: 8/31/70   Round: 1   Board: 2 *

WHITE: *CHESS 3.0*   BLACK: *COKO III*

English Opening

1 P–QB4 (B)   P–K4 (12)   2 N–QB3 (B)   N–QB3 (45)

CHESS 3.0's first two moves were from its book. COKO III did not use a book; Cooper and Kozdrowicki feel that it is not necessary.

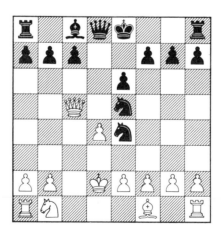

Fig. V-1. *Position after 9 . . . , N–K5+.*

* Time (seconds) spent each move is indicated in parentheses; B is book move.

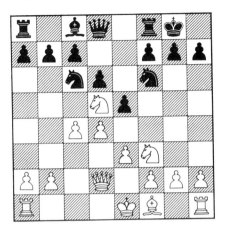

Fig. V-2. *Position after 8 . . . , O–O.*

| 3 N–B3 (71) | B–B4 (21) | 5 P–Q4 (56) | B–QN5 (109) |
| 4 P–K3 (79) | P–Q3 (65) | 6 B–Q2 (73) | . . . |

This prevents Black from giving White an isolated Pawn. As we shall see, CHESS 3.0 is very careful about maintaining good Pawn structure.

6 . . . N–B3 (233)

COKO III takes 4 minutes to decide on this move. No other move by COKO III requires as much time.

| 7 N–Q5 (87) | B × B+ (100) | 8 Q × B (54) | O–O (80) |

(See Fig. V-2.) The next few moves, which characterize computer chess games, result in the dissipation of any tension that exists on the board.

| 9 N × N+ (142) | Q × N (14) | 11 B–Q3 (112) | B–N5 (51) |
| 10 P × P (81) | P × P (17) | 12 B–K4 (93) | . . . |

B–K4 ensures that Black will not weaken White's Pawn structure. Again CHESS 3.0's Pawn structure routine asserts itself.

12 . . . R(R1)–Q1 (45)   13 Q–B2 (104)   P–KR4 (91)

Black finds a simple solution to White's attack on the Rook's Pawn.

14 O–O (63)   B × N (124)   15 B × B (37)   P–R5 (34)

This move is similar in philosophy to 13 . . . , P–KR4. COKO III does not attempt to defend a piece under attack.

16 R(R1)–Q1 (99)   N–N5 (125)   17 Q–K4 (96)   . . .

The next few moves again relieve any tension that exists on the board. Black is left with a weakened Pawn structure.

17 . . .   N × P (86)   19 R × R (28)   Q–QN3 (66)
18 Q × P(N7) (67)   R × R (165)   20 R–R1 (140)   . . .

White cleverly avoids the Queen capture in order to leave Black with isolated pawns.

20 . . .   Q × Q (125)   21 B × Q (30)   R–N1 (3)

From this move until the end of the game, COKO III moves at an average rate of about one move every 15 sec. There are few pieces on the board—both Queens are gone—and COKO III does not have many ideas.

22 R × N (27)   R × B (6)

(See Fig. V-3.)

23 P–B3 (34)   R–N5 (6)   29 K–K1 (32)   R × P(N7) (10)
24 P–B5 (28)   P–QB3 (2)   30 R–B7 (71)   R–N7 (9)
25 P–KN3 (60)   P × P (23)   31 P–N4 (48)   P–K5 (16)
26 P × P (32)   R–QB5 (6)   32 P × P (63)   R × P (13)
27 R × P (41)   R–B8+ (12)   33 R × P(B6) (38)   R × P (3)
28 K–B2 (20)   R–B7+ (9)   34 K–B2 (133)   . . .

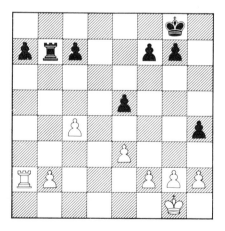

Fig. V-3.   *Position after 22 . . . , R × B.*

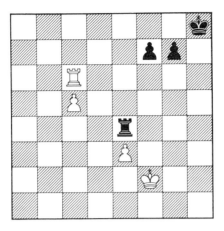

Fig. V-4. *Position after 34 . . . , K–R1.*

CHESS 3.0 takes plenty of time thinking on the next several moves searching for a way to Queen its Bishop's Pawn.

34 . . .   K–R1 (31)

(See Fig. V-4.) The King has gone the wrong way! It should move in the direction of the advanced Bishop's Pawn.

35 R–B8+ (97)   K–R2 (5)   37 K–B3 (482)   . . .
36 P–B6 (226)   P–N4 (26)

The obvious move is 37 P–B7. As is usual in computer chess, weak moves usually take longer to decide on. CHESS 3.0 took 8 minutes to decide on this move, almost twice as long as on any other move.

37 . . .   P–B4 (5)   39 P–B7 (147)   . . .
38 K–B2 (295)   P–B5 (17)

At last!

39 . . .   P × P+ (10)   40 K–K2 (137)   R–K2 (15)

This clinches CHESS 3.0's victory.

41 R–KR8+ (152)   K × R (3)   42 P–B8 = Q (13)   R–K1 (19)

A programming error caused this move to be made.

43 Q × R+ (28)   K–N2 (19)   44 Q–K6 (55)   Resigns

Date: 9/1/70   Round: 2   Board: 1 *

WHITE: *J. Biit* **   BLACK: *CHESS 3.0*

Nimzo-Indian Defense

| 1 P–Q4 | N–KB3 (B) | 3 N–QB3 | B–N5 (63) |
| 2 P–QB4 | P–K3 (B) | 4 P–K3 | B × N+ (27) |

This move is to be expected from CHESS 3.0. It gives J. Biit an isolated Rook's Pawn.

| 5 P × B | N–B3 (97) | 7 P × P | . . . |
| 6 P–Q5 | N–K2 (95) | | |

J. Biit plays into CHESS 3.0's strategy and continues to weaken its own Pawn structure. Berliner suggests 7 P–K4. If 7 . . . , N × P, then 8 Q–N4.

7 . . .   P(B2) × P (46)

(See Fig. V-5.)

8 R–N1	N–B3 (117)	11 B–B5	P–K5 (74)
9 B–Q3	Q–K2 (110)	12 N–Q4	Q–B4 (186)
10 N–B3	P–K4 (141)		

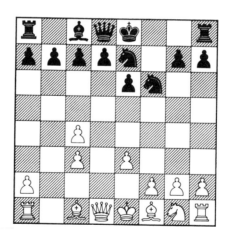

Fig. V-5. *Position after 7 . . . , P(B2) × P.*

---

* Berliner presents an analysis of this game in the *Washington Post* on October, 11, 1970 [3].

** Note: There is no record of the times for White's moves.

This forces J. Biit to give up a Pawn.

13 R–N5	Q × P (75)	16 P(K3) × N	O–O (40)
14 Q–N3	Q × Q (83)	17 O–O	P–QR3 (46)
15 P × Q	N × N (46)	18 R–B5	

J. Biit has made a second serious tactical error. CHESS 3.0 will win a Rook in exchange for a Bishop and a Pawn.

18 . . .	P–Q3 (51)	25 R–Q1	R–B2 (220)
19 B × B	P × R (33)	26 R–Q4	N–B3 (80)
20 B–K6+	K–R1 (12)	27 R–Q2	K–N2 (83)
21 P × P	R(R1)–K1 (76)	28 B–QB4	R(B2)–B1 (59)
22 B–QB4	N–N5 (80)	29 R–Q7+	R–K2 (28)
23 B–K2	N–K4 (86)	30 R × R	. . .
24 B–K3	P–KN3 (196)		

J. Biit trades away its best piece for no compensation. Berliner states that 29 B–Q4+ "gives (White) enough play to draw; the exchange of Rooks is very bad."

30 . . .   N × R (20)

(See Fig. V-6.)

31 B–Q4+   K–R3 (28)   32 B–K5   R–B1 (91)

CHESS 3.0 unnecessarily ties down the Rook. Better was 32 . . . , P–B3.

33 P–R4	P–B3 (84)	36 B–QB4	R–Q8+ (36)
34 B–K6	R–K1 (71)	37 K–R2	N–Q4 (316)
35 B–KB7	R–Q1 (43)	38 P–KN4	P–KN4 (172)

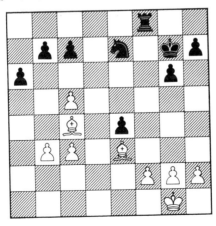

Fig. V-6. *Position after 30 . . . , N × R.*

Black had to prevent White from playing 39 P–N5+, K–R4, 40 B–K2+!

39 P × P+	K × P (86)	42 B–K2	R–Q7 (43)
40 K–R3	N–B5+ (61)	43 B–B1	R × P (37)
41 B × N	K × B (32)	44 B–B4	R–B6+ (49)

(See Fig. V-7.) CHESS 3.0 could have played 44 . . . , P–K6, but it was in no rush to advance the Pawn. This move might be compared with move 37 in the game CHESS 3.0 played with COKO III in Round 1 of the tournament.

45 K–R4	R × P (56)	46 B–N8	P–K6 (196)

CHESS 3.0 takes more than the usual amount of time on this move, plotting strategy for queening the Pawn.

47 B–B4   R × B (226)

Berliner points out that the audience cheered this move.

48 P × R	P–K7 (16)	50 K–R5	Q–KR8 mate (21)
49 P–N5	P–K8 = Q+ (16)		

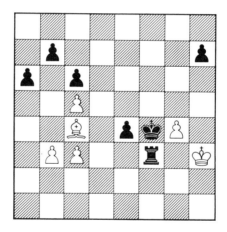

Fig. V-7. *Position after 44 . . . , R–B6+.*

Date: 9/1/70   Round: 2   Board: 2

WHITE: *ĆOKO III*   BLACK: *Daly CP* *

1 P–K4 (7)   P–K3   2 N–QB3 (27)   Q–N4

---

* Note: Black did not provide a record of the times of its moves. At the end of the game Black's clock indicated that 58 minutes were used.

The Black Queen will spend the next three moves looking for a safe square.

3 P–Q4 (25)	Q–R5	6 N–QN5 (110)	B–N5+
4 N–B3 (36)	Q–N5	7 P–B3 (38)	B–R4
5 P–KR3 (47)	Q–R4	8 B–KB4 (231)	P–QR3

A much better move is 8 . . . , P–Q3.

9 N × P+ (31)	B × N	10 B × B (15)	N–QB3

Black might have tried 10 . . . , N–KB3 followed by castling at the first chance.

11 P–Q5 (145)	P × P	13 Q–Q4 (101)	N × P
12 P × P (38)	N(B3)–K2		

This loses the Queen's Knight and leaves Black completely undeveloped after thirteen moves.

14 P–KN4 (55)	Q–N3	17 Q–K5+ (208)	K–B1
15 Q × N (101)	Q–B7	18 B–Q6+ (1)	Resigns
16 B–QB4 (162)	N–R3		

(See Fig. V-8.)

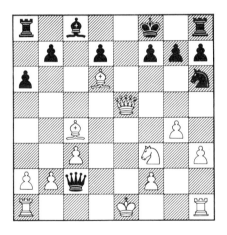

Fig. V-8. *Position at end of game.*

*Date: 9/2/70   Round: 3   Board: 1 **

WHITE: *SCHACH*   BLACK: *CHESS 3.0*

Queen's Gambit Accepted

1 P–Q4   P–Q4   2 P–QB4   P × P

* Neither side provided a record of its move times.

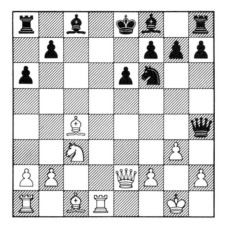

Fig. V-9.   *Position after 12 P–KN3.*

Such a gambit is almost always accepted by a computer chess program. CHESS 3.0 thinks it has won a Pawn and is quite satisfied.

3 N–KB3	N–KB3	7 Q–K2	N–B3
4 P–K3	P–K3	8 N–B3	P × P
5 B × P	P–B4	9 P × P	. . .
6 O–O	P–QR3		

This loses a Pawn. White should have played 9 R–Q1.

9 . . .	N × P	11 R–Q1	Q–R5
10 N × N	Q × N	12 P–KN3	. . .

(See Fig. V-9.) At this point White is in a good position, although down a Pawn. The move 12 . . . , P–KN3 is pointless and only weakens the King's protection. White might have considered 12 B–K3.

12 . . .   Q–N5   13 P–B3   .. . .

Now 13 N–Q5 looks very strong! If 13 . . . , Q × Q, N–B7+, 14 K–K2, B × Q, 15 R–N1, B–KB4, leaving White in a strong position.

13 . . .	B–B4+	16 Q × B	O–O
14 K–R1	Q–N3	17 Q–B5	B–Q2
15 B–K3	B × B	18 P–QR3	. . .

White is getting into trouble by making a number of passive moves.

18 . . .	R(B1)–B1	20 R–Q3	. . .
19 Q–N4	B–B3		

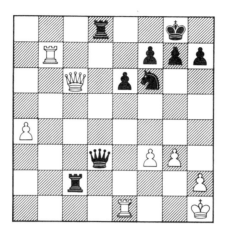

Fig. V-10. *Position after 29 . . . , R–QB7.*

Now White is in serious trouble. If White had played 20 B–K2, its position would have been manageable.

20 . . .	P–N4	24 Q–B4	R × P(N7)
21 N × P	P × N	25 R–N3	R–Q7
22 B × P(N5)	B × B	26 Q–B6	R–K1
23 Q × B	R(B1)–N1		

A wasted move is made by CHESS 3.0.

27 R–K1	R(K1)–Q1	29 P–QR4	R–QB7
28 R–N7	Q–Q6		

(See Fig. V-10.) CHESS 3.0 clinches the victory.

30 Q–N6	Q × P+	31 K–N1	Q–N7 mate

Date: 9/2/70   Round: 3   Board: 2

WHITE: *COKO III*   BLACK: *J. Biit**
Queen's Pawn Game

1 P–Q4 (7)	P–Q4	5 P–QR4 (171)	P–K3
2 N–QB3 (13)	N–QB3	6 N–KB3 (68)	N–B3
3 B–B4 (27)	B–B4	7 P–K3 (201)	N–K5
4 N–N5 (17)	R–B1	8 B–Q3 (351)	B–QN5+

Black's 8 . . . , B–QN5+ wastes a tempo.

* Note: Black did not record its time.

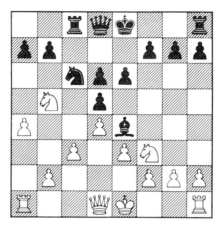

Fig. V-11. *Position after 11 . . . , P × B.*

9 P–B3 (52)   B–Q3   10 B × N (184)   . . .

The next few moves simplify the position.

10 . . .   B × B(K5)   11 B × B (81)   P × B

(See Fig. V-11.)

12 O–O (158)   P–QR3   13 N–R3(3)   . . .

There is only one safe move and COKO III realizes this after just 3 seconds.

13 . . .   O–O   15 P–R5 (66)   N–N1
14 P–QN4 (70)   Q–B3

Much better is 15 . . . , N–K2, followed by N–N3 when the opportunity arises. Black's game would have been much stronger if its Knight were on the King's side. White's Knight is also poorly placed.

16 R–B1 (11)   N–B3

This prevents 17 P–B4.

17 Q–K2 (24)   Q–N3   18 Q–Q1 (107)   . . .

This eliminates the threat of 18 . . . , B–Q6.

18 . . .   B–Q6   21 N–R4 (50)   Q–B3
19 R–K1 (24)   R(KB1)–Q1   22 P–B3 (70)   . . .
20 Q–Q2 (64)   B–K5

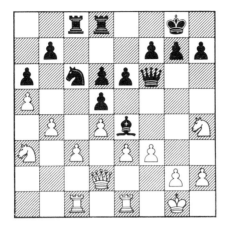

Fig. V-12.   *Position after 22 P–B3.*

(See Fig. V-12.) COKO III characteristically decides to attack the Bishop rather than defend the Knight with 22 P–N3. The four-ply sequence 22 P–B3, Q × N, 23 P × B, Q × P(K5) leads to the loss of a Pawn, but a much deeper search is necessary to see that 22 P–N3 is no better.

22 . . .	Q × N	25 R–B1 (53)	P–B3
23 P–N3 (20)	Q–N4	26 R–B4 (42)	P–Q4
24 P × B (8)	P × P	27 R–R4 (75)	R–B2

The next several moves by White vividly illustrate typical middle-game play by computers when the position is somewhat closed.

28 R–Q1 (88)	R–K2	31 P(K3) × P (48)	P–KN3
29 R–K1 (102)	P–K4	32 N–B2 (138)	P–K6
30 Q–Q1 (27)	P × P		

(See Fig. V-13.) J. Biit cannot hold this Pawn. It would have had a good position with 32 P–B4.

33 Q–B3 (61)   R–K5

J. Biit now will lose two Pawns and give COKO III a slight advantage.

34 R × R (14)	P × R	38 Q–B4 (96)	Q × Q
35 Q × P (K4) (41)	P–B4	39 P × Q (16)	P–R4
36 Q–K6+ (58)	K–N2	40 P–R4 (12)	K–B3
37 Q × P (K3) (68)	Q–N5	41 N–K3 (11)	R–KR1

This move and J. Biit's next move are very weak.

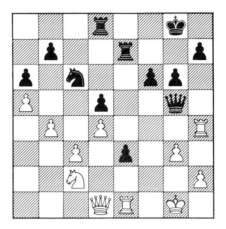

Fig. V-13.   *Position after 32 . . . , P–K6.*

42 P–Q5 (10)   N–R2   43 N–B4 (24)   . . .

Much stronger is 43 P–B4. COKO III's Pawns are not sufficiently aggressive. Also, COKO III's Queen's Bishop's Pawn is vulnerable to attack.

43 . . .   N–N4   44 R–K3 (17)   . . .

Stronger was 44 R–K6+.

44 . . .	R–QB1	48 N–K5+ (38)	K–B1
45 N–N6 (21)	R × P	49 R–KB6+ (32)	K–N2
46 R–K6+ (54)	K–B2	50 R × P(N6)+ (19)	K–R2
47 N–Q7 (44)	N–B2	51 R–N5 (35)	. . .

Again COKO III is not sufficiently aggressive with its Pawns. COKO III would have given J. Biit much more trouble by playing 51 P–Q6.

51 . . .	N × P	62 R–KB5 (62)	K–N3
52 R × P(R5)+ (39)	K–N2	63 R–K5 (47)	R × P
53 R × P(B5) (55)	R–B8+	64 R–QB5 (93)	R–R8+
54 K–R2 (39)	R–B7+	65 K–K2 (31)	R–R7+
55 K–N1 (44)	R–B8+	66 K–K3 (58)	R–R7
56 K–B2 (39)	R–B7+	67 K–B3 (82)	R–R6
57 K–K1 (49)	R–KR7	68 K–K3 (23)	N–N5+
58 R–N5+ (146)	K–R2	69 K–K4 (18)	N–B3+
59 R–R5+ (64)	K–N1	70 K–K3 (22)	N–N5+
60 R–N5+ (64)	K–R2	71 K–K2 (18)	. . .
61 N–Q3 (61)	N–B3		

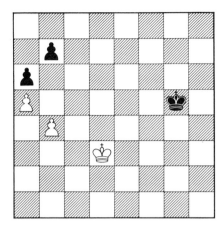

Fig. V-14. *Position after 81 . . . , K × P.*

COKO III avoids a draw.

71 . . .	K–B3	75 K–Q5 (6)	R–Q7
72 R–KN5 (11)	R–R7+	76 K–K4 (10)	R–K7+
73 K–B3 (3)	N–R7+	77 K–Q5 (6)	R–Q7
74 K–K4 (11)	R–K7+	78 K–Q4 (10)	. . .

COKO III again avoids a draw.

78 . . .	N–B6+	80 K × R (6)	N × R
79 K–K3 (29)	R × N+	81 P × N (1)	K × P

(See Fig. V-14.) White can win with either 82 K–Q4 or 82 K–QB4. But COKO III cannot see far enough ahead to realize that it can capture Black's Pawns while saving at least one of its own. A search of about ten plies is necessary to determine this. However, the simple heuristic, "move your King toward Pawns," would have been sufficient to get COKO III's King going in the right direction.

82 K–K3 (1)	K–B4	86 K–K3 (1)	K–Q4
83 K–B3 (1)	K–K4	87 K–Q3 (1)	K–K4
84 K–K3 (1)	K–Q4	Drawn by repetition.	
85 K–Q3 (2)	K–K4		

References

[1] Delvin, John C., Chess computer loses game in a king-size blunder, *The New York Times*, September 2, p. 39 (1970).

[2] Leapman, Michael, Computer wins silver bowl for chess, *The Times* (*London*) September 4, p. 1 (1970).

[3] Berliner, Hans, Berliner on chess, *Washington Post*, October 11 (1970).

[4] Berliner, Hans, United States computer chess championship, *SIGART Newsletter*, ACM, 10–14, December (1970).

[5] Dutka, Jacques, King, Kenneth, and Newborn, Monroe, A review of the first United States computer chess championship, *SIGART Newsletter*, ACM, 14–23, June (1971).

[6] Martin, George R. R., The computer was a fish, *Analog Science Fiction*, August, pp. 61–74 (1972).

[7] "Computer Chess Programs" panel discussion, *Proc. Ann. Conf. ACM 25th*, pp. 97–102 (1971). [Paper presents comments by some of the authors of chess programs participating in the 1971 tournament. Panelists: G. Boos, D. Cooper, J. Gillogly, D. Levy, H. Raymond, D. Slate, R. Smith, B. Mittman (chairman).]

[8] ACM computer chess booklet, distributed at Annual Conf. 1972. [Contains papers describing chess programs of 1972 participants: Newborn and Arnold; Atkin, Gorlen, and Slate; Gillogly; Cooper and Kozdrowicki; Zobrist, Carlson, and Kalme; Smith and Ceruti.]

[9] Berliner, Hans, Experiences gained in constructing and testing a chess program, *IEEE Symp. System Sci. Cybernetics, Pittsburgh, Pennsylvania*, October, 1970.

[10] Kozdrowicki, E., An adaptive tree pruning system: A language for programming tree searches, *Proc. Ann. Conf. ACM 23rd*, pp. 725–735 (1968).

[11] Kozdrowicki, E., Licwinko, J. S., and Cooper, D. W., Algorithms for a minimal chess player: A blitz player, *Int. J. Man-Machine Studies*, 141–165 (1971).

[12] Baylor, G. W.. and Simon, H. A., A chess mating combinations program, *Proc. Spring Joint Computer Conf.*, pp. 431–447, April (1966).

[13] Levy, D. N. L., Computer progress, *Chess*, August, p. 358 (1970). [Presents a game between CHESS 3.0 and a human opponent. The game was played in England; CHESS 3.0 ran on a CDC 6600.]

[14] Smith, Rolf, Jr., The SCHACH chess program, *SIGART Newsletter*, ACM, 8–12, April (1967).

CHAPTER VI

The Second United States Computer Chess Championship (Chicago, 1971)

The second ACM tournament was held at the Chicago Conrad Hilton Hotel, August 2–4, 1971. Computers located as far away as California and New York were tied into the Conrad Hilton by telephone. Professor Mittman organized the event and acquired the services of David Levy [1], an International Master from Scotland, to serve as tournament director. The games were held in the evenings, with play generally starting shortly after 5:30 P.M. Each evening 200–300 people observed the games. Of the eight teams that participated, three were returning for a second shot, while five were newcomers. The three veterans were COKO III, SCHACH, and CHESS 3.5, an improved version of CHESS 3.0.

Berliner went back to Carnegie-Mellon after the 1970 tournament and told his associates that a very simple program using a minicomputer with only 4K of memory had finished second. Professor Allen Newell, Berliner's advisor, upon hearing this, became interested in reconsidering a program based essentially on Turing's ideas. The program would examine *all* possible sequences of moves to some fixed depth and use material on the board along with a limited positional analysis at the first ply as the sole factors in evaluating a position. He felt that this program, with its simple structure, could serve as a "technological benchmark for chess programs which will continue to improve as computer technology increases" [2]. Newell discussed his idea with Jim Gillogly, a graduate student at Carnegie-Mellon, and Gillogly became quite interested. By the time the 1971 Tournament was held, Gillogly was ready with a program that on each move performed an exhaustive search to a depth of three ply and frequently to a depth of four ply. Gillogly's program TECH was the first to come prepared to use its opponent's thinking time to its own advantage. While its opponent was computing a move, TECH would predict what it would be and then proceed to calculate a reply based on the prediction. The predictions, Gillogly claims, are correct about 20% of the time.

The Columbia team of Koenig, Bellovin, Eisenpress, and Yalow was also ready with its program CCCP (Columbia Computer Center Program). They had worked hard throughout the school year and had available the services of the Columbia IBM 360/91. The IBM 360/91 has 1,200,000 bytes of memory, and CCCP used most of it to grow its trees. Most other programs use no more than 10% of this amount of memory space.

Three dark horses also entered: (1) GENIE, written by Captain Herbert Raymond, a US Marine stationed in San Diego, (2) MR. TURK, written by a University of Minnesota team of Gary Boos and James Mundstock, and (3) DAVID, written by Gerhard Wolf of the University of Graz, Austria [3].

In addition to organizing the tournament, Mittman also served as moderator for a panel discussion. Taking part were the authors of the chess programs, Mittman, and Levy. Professor McCarthy was in the audience and contributed to the discussion.

The Tournament*

The first evening of play saw CHESS 3.5 defeat MR. TURK when the latter ran into programming bugs that forced resignation on move 10. COKO III started off well by soundly trouncing CCCP, although the games lasted 50 moves. GENIE won over SCHACH on a time forfeit; it was in a winning position at the end. TECH gained a decisive victory over DAVID and established itself as a contender. TECH won its opponent's Queen on move 17 and maintained a clear lead from there until the end on move 50.

In Round 2, CHESS 3.5 convincingly defeated TECH. CHESS 3.5 was ahead a Bishop for a Pawn by move 20, won another Pawn on move 27, and went into the end game with a Rook advantage. GENIE defeated COKO III after the most incredible game. The latter had mate in one for 8 consecutive moves and refused to make it! DAVID defeated

* See Table VI-1 for the final standings.

SCHACH when the latter ran into technical difficulties while in a lost position; finally, CCCP defeated MR. TURK.

Round 3 provided no surprises. CHESS 3.5 smashed GENIE; GENIE's 17th move led to the loss of its Queen for a Rook and, from there until mate on move 30, there was no question of the outcome. TECH went on to defeat COKO III to assure a second-place tie with GENIE, while CCCP missed its chance to tie for second when, in a won position, it refused to avoid a draw by repetition. Finally, SCHACH defeated trouble-ridden MR. TURK. At a later date, GENIE and TECH had a play-off for second place, which was won by TECH.

TABLE VI-1

Final Standings of the Second United States Computer Chess Championship

Program, authors, computer, location of computer	Round 1	Round 2	Round 3	Points
1. CHESS 3.5 Larry Atkin, Keith Gorlen, David Slate CDC 6400, Northwestern Univ.	W8	W2	W3	3
2. TECH Jim Gillogly PDP-10, Carnegie-Mellon Univ.	W5	L1	W6	2[a]
3. GENIE Herbert Raymond XDS-940, Fleet Computer Center, Pacific, San Diego, California	W7	W6	L1	2
4. CCCP Steven Bellovin, Aron Eisenpress, Andrew Koenig, Benjamin Yalow IBM 360/91, Columbia Univ.	L6	W8	D5	1½
5. DAVID Gerhard Wolf UNIVAC 494, St. Paul, Minnesota	L2	W7	D4	1½
6. COKO III Dennis Cooper, Ed Kozdrowicki UNIVAC 1108, Bell Telephone Laboratories, Piscataway, N.J.	W4	L3	L2	1
7. SCHACH Franklin Ceruti, Rolf Smith UNIVAC 418-III, USAF Communications Computer Programming Center, Oklahoma	L3	L5	W8	1
8. MR. TURK Gary Boos, James Mundstock CDC 6600, Univ. of Minnesota	L1	L4	L7	0

[a] Won a play-off for second place.

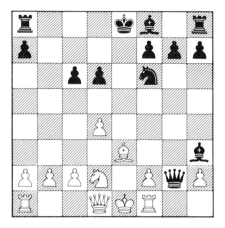

Fig. VI-1. *Position after 10 . . . , P × N.*

Date: August 2, 1971   Round: 1   Board: 2

WHITE: *CCCP**   BLACK: *COKO III*

Petrov's Defense

1 P–K4	P–K4 (14)	4 P–Q4	P–Q3 (168)
2 N–KB3	N–KB3 (171)	5 B–QN5+	P–B3 (91)
3 N × P	Q–K2 (219)	6 B × P+	N × B (4)

After only six moves, it becomes clear that CCCP is in for a tough time.

7 N × N	Q × P+ (8)	9 R–B1	B–R6 (78)
8 B–K3	Q × P(N7) (25)	10 N–Q2	P × N (42)

(See Fig. VI-1.) COKO III has played well and is now a Bishop ahead.

11 Q–B3	Q × Q (71)	13 N–Q2	B × R (2)
12 N × Q	B–N7 (5)		

COKO III wins the exchange after first attempting to capture the Knight.

14 K × B	P–Q4 (30)	15 P–QB4	. . .

CCCP should avoid trading material.

15 . . .	P × P (38)	17 P–KR4	N × B (24)
16 N × P	N–N5 (33)	18 P × N	P–KB4 (27)

* White did not record its time.

COKO III has traded away all the pieces that it had developed.

19 P–R4	B–K2 (16)	21 P–R6	B–N4 (32)
20 P–KR5	P–N3 (51)	22 N–Q6+	. . .

This move is similar in flavor to White's 5 B–QN5+.

22 . . .	K–K2 (38)	24 P–N4	P–B5 (171)
23 N–B4	B × P(R3) (80)	25 P × P	B × P (265)

Every trade is to Black's advantage. Although the game lasts another twenty-one moves, there is little further suspense.

26 R–K1+	K–B3 (184)	33 K–R3	R–B6+ (66)
27 P–N5	R(QR1)–Q1 (117)	34 K–R2	R–Q7+ (255)
28 P × P	R × P (443)	35 K–N1	R–KN6+ (108)
29 N–N2	R–QB1 (63)	36 K–B1	R–KB6+ (114)
30 P–R5	R × P (118)	37 K–N1	R–KN6+ (81)
31 K–N1	B–R7+ (131)	38 K–B1	R–KB6+ (126)
32 K × B	R–B7+ (91)	39 K–N1	R × N (131)

COKO III knows better than to draw.

40 P–R6	R–QR6 (263)	43 K × R	P–R3 (191)
41 R–KB1+	K–N4 (230)	44 K–N2	K–B5 (120)
42 R–B2	R × R (250)		

Does COKO III see mate at this point? Its next two moves are made instantaneously. White can delay mate for a while by playing 45 K–B2 but, instead, makes matters easy for Black.

45 K–R1	K–N6 (1)	46 K–N1	R–R8 mate (1)

(See Fig. VI-2.)

Date: 8/2/71   Round: 1   Board: 4*

WHITE: *TECH*   BLACK: *DAVID*

1 P–K4	P–K3	4 N–B3	Q–R4
2 P–Q4	Q–R5	5 B–Q3	Q–N5
3 N–QB3	N–QB3		

* Neither side provided a record of its time.

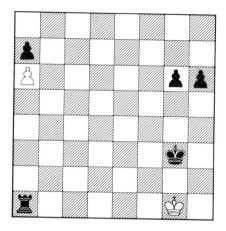

Fig. VI-2.   *Position at end of game.*

Black is looking for trouble by neglecting developing moves.

6 O–O   P–B3   7 B–K3   . . .

(See Fig. VI-3.) TECH always develops its Knights to B3 and its Bishops to B4 or K3 or Q3 if given the chance.

7 . . .	P–QR3	10 P × P	N–Q1
8 Q–K2	P–KN4	11 B–KB4+	N–K2
9 P–Q5	P × P	12 B × P(B7)	P–B4

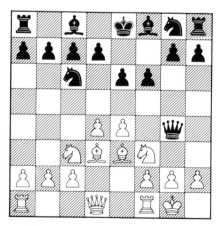

Fig. VI-3.   *Position after 7 B–K3.*

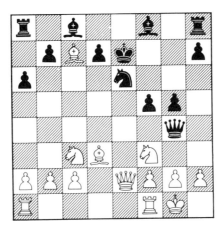

Fig. VI-4. *Position after 14 . . . , K × P.*

Black's game is on the verge of collapse after just twelve moves.

13 P–Q6   N–K3   14 P × N   K × P

(See Fig. VI-4.) Black should have captured with its Bishop. Black now must lose its Queen: 15 N–Q5+, K–K1, 16 N–B6+ winning the Queen or 15 . . . , K–B2, N–K5+ also winning the Queen.

15 N–Q5+   K–K1   17 N × Q   . . .
16 N–B6+   K–B2

Black is now defenseless. For the next 34 moves TECH eagerly exchanges material and finally resorts to queening a Pawn to win the game.

17 . . .	P × N	27 P–KB4	P × P
18 Q–K5	P × N	28 Q × P(B4)	R–N1+
19 Q × R	N × B	29 K–R1	B–Q4+
20 Q × P+	B–N2	30 P–B3	P–N4
21 Q–B5+	B–B3	31 R(B1)–Q1	R–Q1
22 P × P	N–K3	32 Q–B5	B–K3
23 B–B4	P–Q4	33 Q × B(B6)+	K × Q
24 B × P(Q5)	B–Q2	34 R × R	K–K2
25 B × N+	B × B	35 R–K1	. . .
26 Q–K4	R–QN1		

(See Fig. VI-5.) TECH is so eager to exchange material that it is willing to give up a Rook for a Bishop.

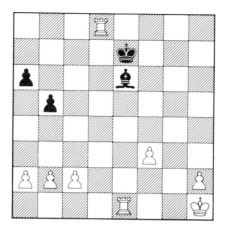

Fig. VI-5. *Position after 35 R–K1.*

35 . . .	K × R	43 K–K4	K–B3
36 R × B	P–R4	44 P–KB5	K–B2
37 R–K5	P–R5	45 K–Q5	K–B1
38 R × P	K–B2	46 P–B6	K–Q2
39 K–N2	K–B3	47 R–N8	P–R6
40 P–QB4	K–B2	48 P–B7	P × P
41 P–B4	K–B3	49 P–B8 = Q	P–N8 = Q
42 K–B3	K–B2	50 Q–N7 mate	

Date: 8/3/71   Round: 2   Board: 1

WHITE: *TECH**   BLACK: *CHESS 3.5*

Sicilian Defense

1 P–K4	P–QB4 (B)	5 N–QB3	P–Q3 (B)
2 N–KB3	N–QB3 (B)	6 B–QB4	P–K3 (B)
3 P–Q4	P × P (B)	7 O–O	P–QR3 (B)
4 N × P	N–B3 (B)	8 B–K3	N–K4 (91)

CHESS 3.5 followed book for the first seven moves.

| 9 Q–K2 | Q–B2 (231) | 10 B–Q3 | . . . |

---

* White did not record its time.

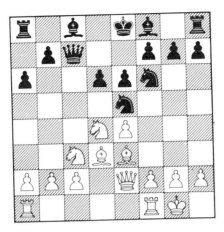

Fig. VI-6. *Position after 10 B–Q3.*

(See Fig. VI-6.) TECH has developed its pieces in almost exactly the same way as it did against DAVID in Round 1.

10 . . .   N(K4)–N5 (150)   11 P–B4   P–K4 (128)

CHESS 3.5 encourages TECH to play 12 P × P isolating White's King's Pawn.

12 N–B5   . . .

TECH encourages its Knights to move from the third to the fifth rank when the opportunity arises.

12 . . .	B–K3 (99)	15 B × B	N–R3 (59)
13 N–Q5	N × N (38)	16 Q–Q3	P–KN3 (32)
14 P × N	B × N (155)	17 B–K4	. . .

TECH does not see that the continuation 17 . . . , P–B4, 18 B–B3, P–K5, leads to a loss of material. The loss occurs too deep in the tree. TECH was probably carrying out an exhaustive 3-ply search and disregarded 17 . . . , B–R3 because of its preference to control the center.

17 . . .   P–B4 (40)   19 Q–Q4   . . .
18 B–B3   P–K5 (27)

TECH might better have traded its lost Bishop for two Pawns: 19 B × P, P × P, 20 Q × P+. Now CHESS 3.5 will win the Bishop for a single Pawn.

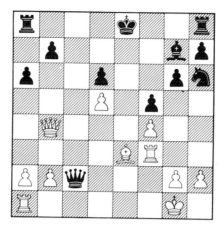

Fig. VI-7. *Position after 21 . . . , Q × P.*

| 19 . . . | B–N2 (32) | 21 R × P | Q × P (107) |
| 20 Q–N4 | P × B (79) | | |

(See Fig. VI-7.) CHESS 3.5 is asking for trouble leaving its Queen's Pawn undefended.

22 Q × P(N7)   . . .

TECH takes the wrong Pawn!

22 . . .   O–O (71)

CHESS 3.5's King scampers to safety.

23 R–B2	Q–Q6 (264)	26 R(Q2)–K2	R(B1)–N1 (78)
24 R–K1	N–N5 (134)	27 Q–Q7	Q × P(Q4) (104)
25 R–Q2	Q–K5 (114)	28 P–QN3	. . .

This leads to loss of the exchange. TECH might have tried 28 R–Q2.

28 . . .	N × B (117)	34 R–K2	Q–Q5+ (33)
29 R × N	B–Q5 (40)	35 K–B3	R–B6+ (34)
30 Q–QB7	B × R+ (53)	36 R–K3	Q–Q8+ (41)
31 R × B	R–QB1 (61)	37 K–B2	Q–Q7+ (31)
32 Q–K7	Q–Q8+ (43)	38 R–K2	Q × P(B5)+ (27)
33 K–B2	R–B7+ (22)		

(See Fig. VI-8.) CHESS 3.5 wins a Pawn while looking for a mate.

39 K–N1	R–B8+ (127)	42 Q × Q	P × Q (9)
40 R–K1	R × R+ (102)	43 K–B2	K–B2 (54)
41 Q × R	Q–K5 (185)	44 K–K3	P–Q4 (34)

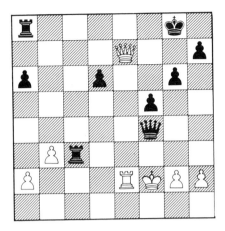

Fig. VI-8.   *Position after 38 . . . , Q × P(B5)+.*

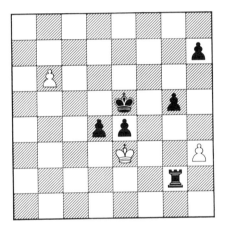

Fig. VI-9.   *Position at end of game.*

Both Kings move towards the center.

45 K–B4	K–K3 (93)	49 P–QN5	P × P (23)
46 P–QN4	R–QB1 (60)	50 P × P	P–N4+ (10)
47 P–KR3	R–B7 (42)	51 K–K3	K–K4 (3)
48 P–QR4	R × P (35)	52 P–N6	P–Q5 mate (1)

(See Fig. VI-9.) TECH backs into checkmate! TECH's heuristic that encourages its King to move towards the center of the board speeds up its
own downfall.

The next game is a classic in the annals of computer chess. From moves 38–45, COKO III has mate in one but refuses to make the move. COKO III has GENIE's King cornered and could mate in one or two; COKO III is as happy with a mate in two as with a mate in one and thus keeps postponing the mate! Fantastic! Meanwhile, GENIE, with nothing better to do, advances a Pawn, finally manages to queen it, and then turns the tables, forcing a resignation from COKO III on move 55.

Date: 8/3/71   Round: 2   Board: 2*

WHITE: *COKO III*   BLACK: *GENIE*

Queen's Pawn Game

1 P–Q4	P–Q4	5 N–K5	B–K3
2 N–KB3	N–KB3	6 N × N	P × N
3 B–N5	B–N5	7 P–QB4	N–Q2
4 N–B3	N–K5		

(See Fig. VI-10.) Black misses 7 . . . , P–KB3. The reader is reminded that GENIE only examines a small number of moves at all plies.

8 N × N	B × N	12 P–Q5	B–N1
9 P–K3	P–KB3	13 Q–B5+	P–K3
10 B–B4	B–K3	14 P × P+	B × P
11 Q–R5+	K–Q2	15 Q × P(K4)	P–QB3

COKO III has clinched the victory after 15 moves.

16 R–Q1+	K–K1	22 Q × P(R7)	B–K2
17 R × Q+	K × R	23 Q–Q3+	K–B1
18 Q × B	B–N5+	24 B–Q6	K–Q2
19 K–K2	R–K1	25 B × B+	K × B
20 Q–N4	P–KN3	26 Q–R7+	. . .
21 Q–R4	P–KN4		

COKO III neglects developing its Bishop and Rook.

26 . . .   K–K3

The King is moving toward the center at the wrong time.

27 Q–K4+   K–Q3   28 P–B5+   . . .

COKO III sacrifices a Pawn possibly in order to bring Black's King out into the open. This may be the influence of MATER.

---

* A record of move times is not available.

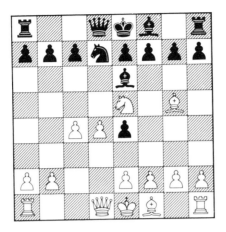

Fig. VI-10. *Position after 7 . . . , N–Q2.*

28 . . .	K × P	31 P–QN4+	K–R5
29 Q–Q4+	K–N4	32 Q–B3	R(R1)–Q1+
30 K–Q1+	K–R4	33 K–B2	R–Q7+

GENIE sees the mate and desperately tries to avoid it. A Rook sacrifice is offered to forestall the doom.

| 34 K × R | R–Q1+ | 36 Q × R | . . . |
| 35 K–B2 | R–Q7+ | | |

(See Fig. VI-11.) Black can no longer prevent White from proceeding with the main theme. White has mate in two. Capturing the Rook with the King would have given White mate in one, but what is the difference at this point?

| 36 . . . | K–R6 | 37 Q–B3+ | K × P |

Now get ready for what follows. Only a computer could do it!

38 K–B1	P–KB4	41 K–B2	P–B6
39 K–B2	P–B5	42 K–B1	P × P
40 K–B1	P–N5	43 K–B2	P × R = Q

COKO III still has mate in one but had better get down to business.

| 44 K–B1 | . . . |

It couldn't happen!

| 44 . . . | Q × B+ | 45 K–Q2 | . . . |

The fatal move is made: Black is back in the ball game! This error in the

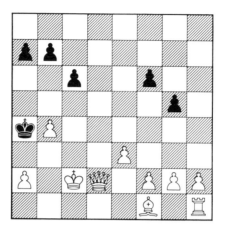

Fig. VI-11.   *Position after 36 Q × R.*

Cooper–Kozdrowicki program can be easily corrected. It is only necessary
to give more credit to mates that occur at early plies in the tree than
to those that occur at deeper plies.

45 . . .	Q × P+		51 Q–B4+	Q–N6
46 K–B1	Q–N8+		52 Q × Q	K × Q
47 K–B2	Q × P(R7)+		53 P–K4	K × P
48 K–B1	Q–R8+		54 P–K5	P–N7
49 K–B2	Q–QN8+		55 Resigns	
50 K–Q2	P–N6			

Date: 8/4/71   Round: 3   Board: 2*

WHITE: *COKO III*   BLACK: *TECH*

Two Knights' Defense

1 P–K4	P–K4		4 P–Q3	P–Q4
2 N–KB3	N–QB3		5 B × P	. . .
3 B–B4	N–B3			

Berliner points out that "5 P × P was necessary. Now Black obtains a
dominant position."

* An analysis of this game by Hans Berliner appears in [2]. Neither side provided a record of its time.

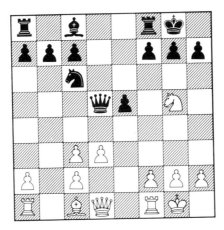

Fig. VI-12. *Position after 10 N–N5.*

5 . . .	N × B	8 O–O	B × N
6 P × N	Q × P	9 P × B	O–O
7 N–B3	B–QN5	10 N–N5	. . .

(See Fig. VI-12.) COKO III could find nothing better. Its moves are made with little consideration for positional value. It might be observed how COKO III's Bishops, Rooks, and Queen remain on the first rank. Meanwhile, TECH has been making good developing moves.

| 10 . . . | B–B4 | 12 P–QB4 | Q–B4 |
| 11 R–N1 | P–B3 | 13 N–R3 | . . . |

Berliner suggests "13 B–K3 and then bring the Knight back to KB3."

13 . . .   B × N

Berliner says that TECH does not recognize doubled Pawns in its scoring function, but probably captured the Knight because it allowed the Bishop to move to a square near the King.

14 B–K3   N–Q5   15 P × B   Q–B3

This defends the Knight's Pawn, relieves the pin on the Knight, and places the Queen on an influential diagonal.

16 P–QB3   . . .

(See Fig. VI-13.) This loses a Rook for a Knight but the exchange occurs at the sixth and seventh plies in the tree and COKO III evidently did not see it. For example, 16 P–QB3, N–B6+; 17 K–R1, N–Q7+; 18 P–B3,

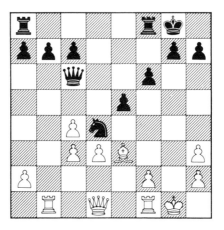

Fig. VI-13. *Position after 16 P–QB3.*

N × R(B8); 19 Q × N. It was necessary for COKO III to play either
16 P–KB3 or 16 B × N in order to avoid 16 . . . , N– B6+.

| 16 . . . | N–B6+ | 18 P–B3 | N × R(B8) |
| 17 K–R1 | N–Q7+ | 19 Q × N | P–B4 |

Berliner credits TECH for "correctly pursuing a policy of gaining space,
but on the next move P–K5 is better."

| 20 R–N5 | P–B5 | 22 B–B1 | P–B3 |
| 21 R–B5 | Q–K3 | 23 P–Q4 | R(R1)–K1 |

Berliner attributes this move to a programming bug and suggests that
23 . . . , "P × P wins."

| 24 R × P(K5) | Q–N3 | 26 Q–B2 | . . . |
| 25 R × R | Q × R | | |

For the next several moves, COKO III is at a loss for ideas. There are
no pieces to attack, and none of its own pieces are under attack.

| 26 . . . | Q–K3 | 28 P–KR4 | P–B4 |
| 27 Q–B1 | R–B4 | | |

Berliner says that "it is interesting that this important strategic break
comes as a result of the positional heuristics, since there is no material
gain involved."

| 29 P–Q5 | Q–Q3 | 31 Q–B1 | . . . |
| 30 Q–R3 | Q–K4 | | |

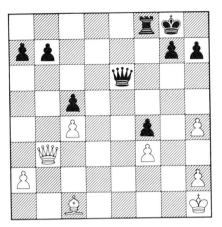

Fig. VI-14. *Position after Q–N3.*

COKO III makes it easier for TECH by wasting moves with its Queen. After 31 moves, COKO III still has all pieces, except for Pawns, on the first rank.

31 . . .	Q × P(B6)	35 Q–R4	R–B4
32 P–Q6	Q–Q5	36 Q–K8+	R–B1
33 Q–K2	Q × P(Q3)	37 Q–R4	Q–K3
34 Q–K8+	R–B1		

TECH avoids a draw.

38 Q–N3   . . .

(See Fig. VI-14.)

38 . . .   Q–K7

This threatens mate in one and also keeps open the option of winning the Bishop.

39 P–KR3	R–Q1	41 Resigns
40 B × P	R–Q8+	

*Date: 8/4/71   Round: 3   Board: 3**

WHITE: *CCCP*   BLACK: *DAVID*

1 P–K4	P–K3	5 B × N	P(Q2) × B
2 P–Q4	N–QB3	6 B–K3	P–N4
3 N–QB3	P–KN4	7 Q–R5	P–QN5
4 B–N5	P–QR3		

* Neither side provided a record of its time.

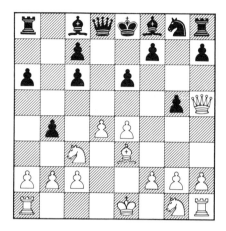

Fig. VI-15. *Position after 7 . . . , P–QN5.*

(See Fig. VI-15.) This results in the loss of a Pawn for Black.

8 B × P   N–B3

If 8 . . . , Q × P, then 9 R–Q1.

9 B × N   Q × B   10 P–K5   . . .

This gets White into trouble. CCCP should have played 10 N(B3)–K2.

10 . . .	Q–N2	14 N–B6+	K–K2
11 N–K4	Q × P(N7)	15 P–QR3	P × P
12 Q–B3	Q × Q	16 R × P	R–QN1
13 N × Q	B–R3	17 O–O	. . .

CCCP overlooks 17 . . . , R × P.

17 . . .   R × P   18 P–B4   P–R4

DAVID gives up a Pawn in return.

19 R × P	R–N6	21 K × R	. . .
20 K–N2	R × N		

Black is now in a weak position. White's Rooks have good mobility and its Pawns are very strong.

21 . . .	B–Q7	23 R × P	. . .
22 R–B5	B–B6		

White plays a very clever sequence!

23 . . .   B–N2

This pins the Rook.

24 N–Q5+   . . .

This relieves the pin.

24 . . .	P × N	30 R–B5+	K–R3
25 R × P+	K–K3	31 R–B6+	K–R4
26 R × B	P × P	32 R–B5+	K–R3
27 R–N6+	K–B4	33 R–B6+	K–R4
28 R–KB6+	K–N4	34 R–B5+	Drawn by repetition.
29 R–N1+	K–R4		

White has not been taught to avoid draws by repetition when in a clearly won position.

*Date: September, 1971   Playoff for second place**

WHITE: *GENIE*   BLACK: *TECH*

Ruy Lopez

1 P–K4	P–K4	5 N–B3	P–Q3
2 N–KB3	N–QB3	6 P–Q4	P × P
3 B–N5	N–B3	7 N × P	B–Q2
4 O–O	B–B4	8 N–B5	O–O

(See Fig. VI-16.) TECH has completed its initial development and will now attempt to gain greater control of the center.

9 B–N5   N–K4   10 N–QR4   . . .

GENIE, searching a smaller tree than TECH, is evidently not able to see the consequences of this weak move.

10 . . .	B × B	14 N × P	P × N
11 N × B	B × R	15 B × N	P × B
12 N × P(QN7)	Q–N1	16 Q × B	. . .
13 N–K7+	K–R1		

(See Fig. VI-17.) TECH emerges from this slugfest with a Rook for two Pawns.

| 16 . . . | Q–N5 | 18 N × P | Q × P(B7) |
| 17 N–Q5 | Q × P(K5) | 19 Q–B1 | Q × Q+ |

* The only available record of the time used by each side is incomplete and inexact.

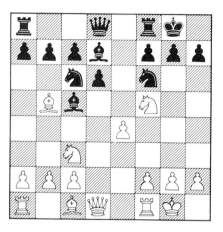

Fig. VI-16. *Position after 8 . . . , O–O.*

TECH is eager to exchange material.

| 20 R × Q | K–N2 | 22 N–B4+ | K–B4 |
| 21 N–R5+ | K–N3 | 23 N–Q5 | R(R1)–Q1 |

TECH encourages its Rooks to get behind passed Pawns. In this case the tactic is of no particular consequence.

| 24 R–K1 | R–QN1 | 26 R–K2 | N × P(N5) |
| 25 P–QN4 | N–Q6 | 27 N–B3 | R(B1)–K1 |

TECH is still eager to exchange material.

| 28 P–QR3 | R × R | 29 N × R | N–Q4 |

(See Fig. VI-18.) TECH threatens mate in one. Better is 29 . . . , N–B7 threatening mate and also winning the Rook's Pawn. TECH requires 30 additional moves to clinch the victory. Fifteen moves are made before TECH realizes that it is necessary to advance its Pawns.

30 P–KR4	K–K5	34 N–N3	K × P
31 P–R5	R–Q1	35 P–R4	K–B6
32 P–R6	R–QB1	36 P–R5	R–KN1
33 P–N4	K–B6	37 P–R6	R × N+

TECH is willing to exchange a Rook for a Knight and a Pawn.

38 P × R	K × P	42 K–Q4	K–B5
39 K–B1	N–N5	43 K–Q5	N–K5
40 K–K2	N × P	44 K–B6	K–K4
41 K–K3	N–B4	45 K–N7	P–R4

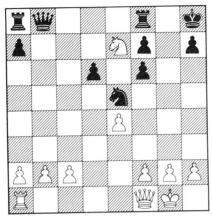

Fig. VI-17. *Position after 16 Q × B.*

GENIE is unaware that it should avoid encouraging TECH's Pawn to move.

46 K–B6	P–R5		50 K–K7	Q–QB8
47 K–Q7	P–R6		51 K–Q7	Q × P
48 K–K7	P–R7		52 K–B6	Q–K6
49 K × P	P–R8 = Q		53 K–B7	P–Q4

One Queen isn't enough!

54 K–B6	P–Q5		57 K–Q7	P–Q8 = Q+
55 K–Q7	P–Q6		58 K–B6	Q–R2
56 K–B6	P–Q7		59 K–N5	Q(Q8)–R5 mate

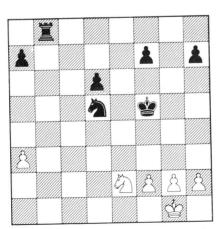

Fig. VI-18. *Position after 29 . . . , N–Q4.*

References

[1] Levy, D. N. L., Computer chess—a case study on the CDC 6600, *Machine Intelligence*, 151–163 (1971).

[2] James Gillogly, The technology chess program, *Artificial Intelligence* (3), 145–163 (1972).

[3] "Computer Chess Programs" (panel discussion), *Proc. Ann. Conf. ACM 24th*, pp. 98–113 (1971). [Articles by H. Raymond, J. Gillogly, D. Slate, G. Boos, R. Smith, and D. Cooper.]

CHAPTER VII

The Third United States Computer Chess Championship (Boston, 1972)

For the third consecutive year, the program of Larry Atkin, Keith Gorlen, and David Slate captured the United States Computer Chess Championship. Again the ACM hosted the three-round Swiss-system tournament, this time at the Sheraton-Boston Hotel on the dates of August 13–15, 1972. As in 1971, eight programs participated and, as in 1971, David Levy acted as tournament director. The usual crowds of 200 to 300 persons observed play each evening. The tournament received wide news coverage including an analysis of one of the games by Samuel Reshevsky [1, 2, 3, 9]. (See Table VII-1 for final standings.)

Of the eight programs that participated, four were the work of authors who had competed in previous tournaments. There was the updated version of last year's winning program, now called CHESS 3.6. There was also an improved version of TECH, the runner-up in 1971. Gillogly had refined TECH's tree-searching heuristics to the point where the program was able to search between 1 and 2 plies deeper than in 1971. Gillogly's program appeared to have the best chance to upset CHESS 3.6. Cooper and Kozdrowicki had not had the opportunity to make any major improvements in COKO III and returned with essentially the same program as in 1971. This was also the case with Ceruti and Smith, who had not made any significant changes in SCHACH for almost two years.

There were four newcomers. Frederic Carlson, Charles Kalme, and Al Zobrist, members of the faculty of the University of Southern California, had developed a program that the authors contend was based on a philosophically different approach than the other programs. The USC program uses a scoring function that gives credit for having certain "patterns" present on the board. At the time of the tournament, the program searched for about 45 different patterns. The program is structured so that additional patterns can be easily added by a chess player unfamiliar with the details of the program [5, 8].

OSTRICH, the product of George Arnold and the author, also entered (it is described in Chapter X). Data General provided us with a Nova 800 computer in Boston, and it became the second computer to be at the site of an ACM tournament. The Nova 800 is essentially identi-

TABLE VII-1

Final Standings of the Third United States Computer Chess Championship

Program, authors, computer, location of computer	Round			Points
	1	2	3	
1. CHESS 3.6; Larry Atkin, Keith Gorlen, David Slate; CDC 6400, Northwestern Univ.	W2	W4	W3	3
2. OSTRICH; George Arnold, Monty Newborn; Data General Nova 800, at site of the tournament	L1	W7	W6	2[a]
3. TECH; Jim Gillogly; PDP–10, Carnegie-Mellon Univ.	W6	W5	L1	2
4. COKO III; Dennis Cooper, Ed Kozdrowicki; UNIVAC 1108, Bell Telephone Laboratories Whippany, N.J.	W7	L1	W5	2
5. The USC CP; Albert Zobrist, Fredric Carlson, Charles Kalme; IBM 370/155, USC, Los Angeles	W8	L3	L4	1
6. SCHACH; Rolf Smith, Franklin Ceruti; IBM 360/65, Texas A&M	L3	W8	L2	1
7. The MSU CP; Mike Rackley, George Moore; UNIVAC 1106, Mississippi State Univ.	L4	L2	D8	½
8. The Leverett CP; Bruce Leverett; PDP-10, Harvard Univ.	L5	L6	D7	½

Results of play-off for second place

	OSTRICH	TECH	COKO III	Points
OSTRICH	×	1	1	2
TECH	0	×	1	1
COKO III	0	0	×	0

[a] Won a three-way play-off for second place.

cal to the Supernova used at Columbia while developing the program [5]. The other two entries were the Mississippi State University program, written by George Moore and Michael Rackley, and the Leverett CP, written by Bruce Leverett, a student at Harvard University. Of the four newcomers, the USC CP and OSTRICH were expected to perform creditably, while the other two had been developed just prior to the tournament and were not expected to provide serious threats.

The Tournament*

CHESS 3.6 won the tournament by winning three straight games, extending the perfect record of Atkin, Gorlen, and Slate's program to nine consecutive victories in the ACM tournaments (see Table VII-1 for the final standings). However, their program met stiffer competition than it had in the previous two years, as indicated by the lengths of the games played. Its first victory required 77 moves, its second 72, and its third 51. In the previous two years CHESS 3.0's and CHESS 3.5's opponents lasted an average of only 36 moves. Atkin, Gorlen, and Slate had hoped to introduce sweeping changes in CHESS 3.5, planning to call the new version CHESS 4.0. However, because they found themselves short of time, they made only several minor modifications and decided to rename their program simply CHESS 3.6.

In each victory CHESS 3.6 resorted to the threat of queening a Pawn or the actual queening of a Pawn to clinch its victories. It excelled in provoking Pawn weaknesses and then pushing its Pawns on the weakened side. CHESS 3.6's play was also positionally stronger than its opponents. In the first round OSTRICH gave CHESS 3.6 an anxious moment or two when OSTRICH played 29 . . . , Q–N4. However CHESS 3.6 played well and OSTRICH was unable to sustain the pressure. Again, in Round 2, CHESS 3.6 found itself in trouble and in a drawn game with COKO III, but COKO III did not realize that its King had to move towards its opponent's Pawns in order to force the draw. COKO III's King went the wrong way, and CHESS 3.6 went on to win. Its win over TECH in Round 3 was an interesting game in which positional play was a major factor.

The three rounds ended with three teams tied for second place: OSTRICH, TECH, and COKO III all finished with two points. A three-way play-off was arranged at midnight on the last night of the tournament. The first game took place between OSTRICH and TECH, beginning that evening at about 1 A.M. and ending at about 4 A.M. when

* See Newborn [4].

TECH lost on time. The second game between TECH and COKO III was started September 28 and was completed one week later. TECH emerged victorious after 145 moves and after evading a draw by repetition 12 times! OSTRICH gained the runner-up position by defeating COKO III on November 18.

System difficulties and programming errors played only a small part in the tournament. Leverett's program ran into difficulties in Round 2. Leverett used a PDP 10 at the Harvard Computation Center for Rounds 1 and 3 but was forced to use a local time-sharing service for Round 2. The time-sharing service became heavily loaded around 8 P.M. and caused his program to lose on time. The only other major technical difficulty was experienced by the USC CP, which was forced to stop its third-round game with COKO III at 10 P.M., August 15, because the IBM 360/155 computer at USC was needed for other purposes. It was in a lost position at the time.

To date, two minicomputers have participated in the ACM tournaments and both have fared quite well. Clearly the Data General Nova or Supernova, with 16,000 words of memory, is sufficiently large and fast to compete on an equal basis with larger computers.

On the morning of the last day of the tournament the authors of the programs met for a panel discussion. Professor Mittman served as moderator. Other members of the panel were David Levy, Jim Gillogly, Al Zobrist, George Arnold, Franklin Ceruti, David Slate, Ed Kozdrowicki, and the author. The panel arrived at few conclusions: (1) a need for including algorithms controlling long-range strategy was emphasized; (2) there was interest in the USC approach; (3) self-learning by chess programs was confirmed as being a long way off. Arthur Samuel was in the audience and participated actively in the discussion [6, 7].

Date: 8/13/72   Round: 1   Board:1

WHITE: *CHESS 3.6*   BLACK: *OSTRICH*

Sicilian Defense

1 P–K4 (B)	P–QB4 (B)	4 N × P (B)	P–K4 (B)
2 N–KB3 (B)	N–QB3 (B)	5 N–KB3 (235)	Q–N3 (B)
3 P–Q4 (B)	P × P (B)		

White played from book for the first four moves, Black for the first five. It might be noted that the times for both White's and Black's first moves out of book were relatively long when compared with the next few moves. The book openings left both computers in somewhat unnatural positions

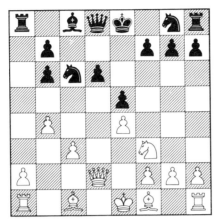

Fig. VII-1. *Position after 11 . . . , P × N.*

and the first moves out of book were attempts to convert to more natural ones. OSTRICH has this irregular move 5 . . . , Q–N3 in its book because it was felt that this move would give Black a somewhat aggressive game.

6 N–B3 (140)   B–B4 (269)   7 Q–Q2 (199)   P–Q3 (227)

Better for Black was 7 . . . , N–B3 to stall White's 8 N–Q5.

8 N–Q5 (181)   Q–Q1 (144)   9 P–QN4 (74)   B–Q5 (143)

9 . . . , B–Q5 qualifies as an OSTRICH move, since it delays the forced move B–N3 as long as possible.

10 P–B3 (64)   B–N3 (147)   11 N × B (49)   P × N (44)

(See Fig. VII-1.) CHESS 3.6 has succeeded at its favorite tactic—doubling and isolating its opponent's Pawns. It now has a good target: Black's weak Pawns in the Queen's Knight's file.

12 B–B4 (99)   B–K3 (207)   13 B × B (69)   P × B (39)

OSTRICH asks for trouble!

14 N–N5 (92)   Q–Q2 (87)   16 N–B3 (56)   O–O–O (220)
15 O–O (115)   P–KR3 (58)

OSTRICH's scoring function encourages castling without sufficiently weighting the safety of the King in its new position.

17 R–Q1 (65)   N–B3 (245)

A long series of moves follows during which neither side exhibits any direction or plan. Obviously White should plan a Queen's-side Pawn attack supported by its Rooks and Queen, while Black must press on the King's side.

18 Q–K2 (115)   Q–QB2 (230)   20 N–Q2 (135)   P–Q4 (67)
19 B–N2 (108)   N–K2 (195)   21 P–QB4 (95)   . . .

If Black captures with 21 . . . , P × P(B5), then 22 N × P leaves Black with a very poor Pawn structure. Black's 21 . . . , P × P(K5) is bad for the same reason.

21 . . .   P–Q5 (246)   22 Q–Q3 (91)   N–N3 (154)

Black might have had a much stronger game on the King's side if it had played 22 . . . , P–KN4 followed by N–KN3 and then N–KB5 later.

23 P–N3 (119)   Q–K2 (162)   24 B–R3 (70)   K–B2 (90)

This move is the first of several King moves and Rook moves by Black that gradually lead to its downfall. This sort of position is, of course, a difficult one for a computer since there is nothing that can be accomplished tactically to the immediate advantage of either side.

25 R(R1)–N1 (122)   R–R2 (257)

White's move is weak but Black's is weaker yet. White could have played 25 R(Q1)–QB1 followed by P–B5, giving it a strong attack. Black's move was probably the result of finding nothing better to do than to advance a piece; OSTRICH gives a little credit for advancing pieces.

26 R–K1 (88)   R–Q2 (89)

Again, both sides make weak moves.

27 K–N2 (75)   Q–Q1 (69)   28 P–R3 (80)   N–N1 (257)

OSTRICH had a programming error in its move-timing routine that showed up during this game. It was corrected for the later rounds. The readers can note that most moves are made alternately in times around either 250 or 60 sec. Essentially on every other move OSTRICH searches a tree of different depth: on one move the depth (DMIN) is four ply; on the next move DMIN is five ply (see pp. 163–165 in Chapter X).

29 R–N3 (94)   Q–N4 (63)

(See Fig. VII-2.) White has played rather passively for the last ten moves or so and Black has maneuvered into an attacking position threatening 30 . . . , N–B5+. During the next several moves Black's position reaches its pinnacle; after move 33 it gradually deteriorates.

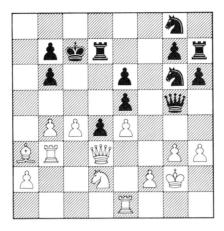

Fig. VII-2. *Position after 29 . . . , Q–N4.*

30 K–R2 (115)   R–B2 (249)

Black has deserted its King! But White has a few of its own problems.

31 Q–K2 (101)   N–B3 (94)   33 P–R4 (80)   N–N5+ (249)
32 R–KB3 (130)   P–R4 (63)

(See Fig. VII-3.) Black ignores the continuation 33 . . . , N × P(R5); 34
P × P, Q × P+, leading to the exchange of a Knight for two Pawns. If
35 K–N1 or K–N2, then 35 . . . , Q–N5+; 36 K–B1, and Black has not
gained enough compensation for its Knight.

34 K–R1 (88)   Q–K2 (78)   36 N × R (65)   Q–B3 (52)
35 K–N2 (110)   R × R (216)   37 B–B1 (108)   K–Q3 (251)

Black invites trouble.

38 B–N5 (106)   Q–B2 (63)

Black apparently missed the move 39 B–Q8 at the second ply in its move
tree. White has 36 moves in this position, and as a result of forward
pruning Black considered successors of only about 18 of them.

39 B–Q8 (176)   R–R1 (286)   42 P–N5 (185)   Q–QB1 (111)
40 B × P (157)   K–K2 (63)   43 R–QN1 (195)   R–B1 (82)
41 N–N5 (97)   Q–K1 (243)   44 R–KB1 (94)   R–K1 (335)

This move, which is quite weak, takes Black more time to select than any
other move. Once again we see that the longer a move takes to decide
upon, the worse the move!

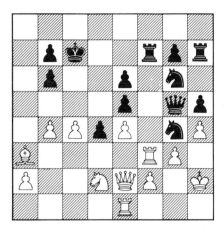

Fig. VII-3. *Position after 33 . . . , N–N5+.*

| 45 Q–B3 (173) | R–B1 (135) | 47 B–B5 (135) | R–R1 (94) |
| 46 Q–R3+ (78) | K–Q2 (82) | | |

White is gradually strengthening its position.

48 N–B7 (146)	R–R2 (104)	52 R–K1 (149)	R–R1 (126)
49 R–B1 (155)	N–R3 (88)	53 K–N1 (36)	N–N5 (116)
50 N–Q6 (26)	Q–B2 (234)	54 R–KB1 (110)	R–R3 (299)
51 P–N6 (110)	Q–B3 (69)		

(See Fig. VII-4.) White has played a series of passive moves but Black, once again, outdoes White in this respect with 54 . . . , R–R3.

55 N–B7 (99)	Q × P(K5) (151)	60 K–N2 (109)	N–B4 (232)
56 N× R (106)	N × N (75)	61 K–B2 (100)	Q–B1 (232)
57 P–B3 (56)	Q–B3 (102)	62 R–N5 (88)	K–Q2 (99)
58 K–B2 (67)	K–Q1 (128)	63 R–N2 (78)	K–B3 (288)
59 R–QN1 (96)	Q–Q2 (119)		

White's move 62 R–N5 evoked cheers from the weary spectators; the move 63 R–N2 brought hisses! At this point White is an exchange ahead with mating possibilities. But White is playing very passively, giving Black all possible chances.

64 Q–N4 (234)	K–Q2 (80)	67 P × Q (39)	K–Q1 (60)
65 Q–N5+ (80)	Q–B3 (39)	68 R–Q3 (74)	N(N3)–K2 (165)
66 R–Q2 (85)	Q × Q (227)		

At last, White will force victory by advancing its Pawns.

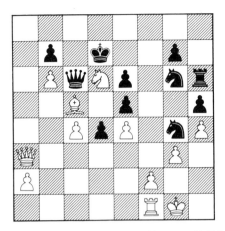

Fig. VII-4. *Position after 54 . . . , R–R3.*

69 P–R4 (129)	P–N3 (66)	74 R–R3 (52)	K–R1 (85)
70 P–R5 (79)	K–Q2 (211)	75 P–N7+ (27)	K × P (1)
71 P–R6 (50)	P × P (57)	76 P–R8=Q+ (32)	K–B2 (1)
72 P × P (138)	K–B1 (231)	77 R–R7 mate (32)	
73 P–R7 (105)	K–N2 (129)		

Date: 8/13/72   Round: 1   Board: 2

WHITE: *SCHACH*   BLACK: *TECH*

Queen's Gambit Accepted

1 P–Q4 (B)   P–Q4 (2)   2 P–QB4 (B)   P × P (5)

A computer always accepts a gambit. White is not clever enough to win
the Pawn back. SCHACH played the same opening against CHESS 3.0
in the 1970 United States Computer Chess Championship (Round 3,
Board 1) and was allowed to recapture the Pawn but will not be able
to do so this time.

3 N–KB3 (B)   N–QB3 (10)

This move can get Black into trouble.

4 P–K4 (72)   P–QN4 (1)   5 P–Q5 (174)   N–N5 (25)

White is now in a position to make Black pay for its weak third move. But
White is not sufficiently strong.

6 B–N5 (133)   N–KB3 (358)   8 B–K2 (187)   B–QB4 (253)
7 B × N (211)   P(K2) × B (269)

The reader should note three characteristics of Gillogly's program that this game illustrates very well: (1) its desire to control and occupy center squares, (2) its desire to trade material when ahead, and (3) its ability to think on the opponent's time. Fifteen of the 63 moves are made by TECH in 1 sec, indicating that it anticipated its opponent's reply at least 24% of the time. TECH may have anticipated its opponent's response to a few other moves but did not have time to complete the calculation of its own move before its opponent responded.

9 N–B3 (101)   B–Q2 (261)   10 O–O (157)   O–O (104)

(See Fig. VII-5.)

11 N–KR4 (175)   Q–K2 (311)   14 N–K3 (142)   P–B3 (648)
12 P–QR3 (265)   N–R3 (150)   15 P × P (248)   B × P (402)
13 N–B5 (195)   Q–K4 (1)

TECH's last two moves consumed over 17 minutes. Its fifteenth move, which was a relatively obvious move, required almost 7 minutes. TECH's weak control over the size of the tree that is searched leads to trouble in two games in later rounds.

16 N × P(B4) (204)   P × N (42)

It is a more common occurrence in computer chess than in human chess that a Knight is traded for two Pawns—especially if the Pawns are middle

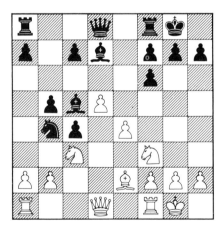

Fig. VII-5.   *Position after 10 . . . , O–O.*

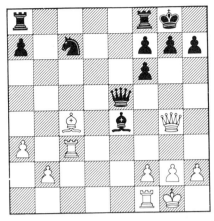

Fig. VII-6. *Position after 20 . . . , B × P.*

Pawns. One might give SCHACH the benefit of the doubt here and propose that its scoring function was slightly out of line, thus leading to this exchange. The other possibility is that SCHACH, since it looks at only captures plus six or seven moves in each position, could find nothing better.

17 B × P (153)   N–B2 (315)

Black's Knight is forced to find a good square. At this point TECH is ahead a Knight for a Pawn.

18 Q–N4 (157)   B–Q5 (367)   20 R × B (121)   B × P (1)
19 R(R1)–B1 (284)   B × N (381)

(See Fig. VII-6.) TECH is a Knight ahead and eager to trade material.

21 R–K1 (177)   B–B6 (108)   23 R–K7 (75)   N–K3 (1)
22 R × Q (125)   B × Q (1)   24 B × N (93)   B × B (42)

TECH, when given the choice, seems to prefer to capture with pieces other than its own Pawns. In this case, however, by capturing with the Bishop, TECH increases its center control.

25 P–KN3 (220)   R(B1)–K1 (93)   30 K–B2 (95)   K–B1 (1)
26 R × R (50)   R × R (1)   31 P–QN4 (121)   R–K3 (343)
27 R–B7 (60)   B–Q4 (78)   32 R–Q8+ (78)   K–K2 (39)
28 P–B4 (106)   P–QR3 (50)   33 R–Q1 (96)   R–Q3 (142)
29 R–Q7 (41)   B–K5 (39)   34 R–K1 (78)   . . .

This is the first time that SCHACH has avoided a trade.

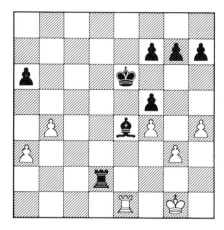

Fig. VII-7.   *Position after 36 P–KR4.*

34 . . .   R–Q7+ (191)   36 P–KR4 (56)   . . .
35 K–N1 (125)   P–B4 (191)

(See Fig. VII-7.) This error by SCHACH makes TECH's win easier.

36 . . .   R–KN7+ (963)

TECH takes 15 minutes to decide on this obviously strong move!

37 K–B1 (54)	R × P (1)	44 K–B2 (30)	B–Q4 (85)
38 P–R4 (58)	R–N6 (1)	45 K–K3 (19)	K–Q3 (63)
39 P–KR5 (209)	R × P (44)	46 K–Q4 (20)	B–K3 (78)
40 P–R5 (46)	R–N8 (1)	47 K–Q3 (34)	B–R7 (548)
41 K–B2 (110)	R × R (40)	48 K–Q4 (47)	B–Q4 (370)
42 K × R (49)	B–B6 (1)	49 K–K3 (72)	K–B3 (941)
43 P–R6 (62)	P × P (52)	50 K–Q4 (45)	P–R4 (1)

(See Fig. VII-8.) TECH finally finds the way to victory. Its behavior can be seen to be consistent with that exhibited in its game with GENIE in the Second United States Computer Chess Championship.

51 K–K5 (49)	B–K5 (1)	53 K–K5 (22)	P–R6 (1)
52 K–Q4 (25)	P–R5 (1)	54 K–Q4 (24)	K–N4 (98)

TECH sees that it can queen the Pawn, but also sees that it can grab a free Pawn before continuing with the main theme.

55 K–K5 (43)	K × P (175)	57 K–K5 (46)	P–R8 = Q (764)
56 K–Q4 (34)	P–R7 (54)	58 K–Q4 (87)	P–R3 (1265)

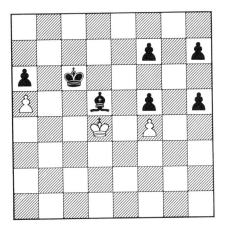

Fig. VII-8. *Position after 50 . . . , P–R4.*

TECH takes 20 minutes to select this move! Gillogly thought his computer had broken down.

59 K–K5 (68)	Q–R5 (2)	62 K–Q8 (58)	P–KR4 (46)
60 K–Q6 (49)	Q × P+ (2)	63 Resigns	
61 K–Q7 (63)	K–N3 (11)		

Date: 8/14/72   Round: 2   Board: 1

WHITE: *COKO III*   BLACK: *CHESS 3.6*

Queen's Pawn Game

1 P–Q4 (11)	P–Q4 (B)	3 N–B3 (10)	B–N5 (80)
2 N–QB3 (19)	N–KB3 (B)		

The motivation for several of CHESS 3.6's next few moves is clearly related to its favorite tactic: preserve good Pawn structure.

4 Q–Q3 (23)   . . .

COKO III is too eager to involve the Queen in the fight.

4 . . .	N–B3 (137)	6 B–N5 (250)	N–QN5 (83)
5 N–K5 (169)	B–Q2 (165)	7 Q–Q1 (245)	. . .

COKO III admits its fourth move was a mistake. 7 Q–Q2 would have given COKO III more mobility.

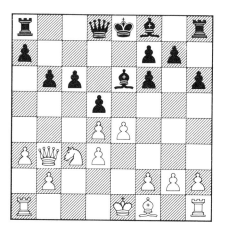

Fig. VII-9. *Position after 13 . . . , P–B3.*

7 . . .	B–B4 (69)	11 P(B2) × N (93)	B–K3 (67)
8 N–Q3 (143)	P–KR3 (97)	12 Q–N3 (29)	P–QN3 (38)
9 B × N (50)	P(K2) × B (46)	13 P–K4 (47)	P–B3 (37)
10 P–QR3 (130)	N × N (48)		

(See Fig. VII-9.) Black cannot play 13 . . . , P × P because of 14 P–Q5. CHESS 3.6's move results in a weakening of COKO III's Pawn structure.

14 Q–R4 (92)	Q–Q2 (65)	17 R–B1 (148)	K–Q2 (117)
15 P × P (43)	B × P(Q4) (36)	18 Q–B4 (224)	B–Q3 (134)
16 N × B (73)	Q × N (59)		

CHESS 3.6 is gradually building up a small positional advantage. COKO III continues to overuse its Queen, neglecting other moves.

19 Q × Q (76)	P × Q (36)	21 P–QR4 (37)	P–B4 (38)
20 B–K2 (21)	R(QR1)–K1 (114)	22 P–QN3 (27)	. . .

(See Fig. VII-10.) COKO III has sealed the fate of its Pawn on Q4, although CHESS 3.6 takes another eight moves before finally capturing it.

22 . . .	B–N5+ (44)	27 K–Q1 (16)	B–B6 (76)
23 K–Q1 (24)	R–QB1 (57)	28 P–KN4 (14)	P × P (36)
24 R × R (28)	R × R (29)	29 B × P(N4) (5)	P–N3 (58)
25 B–B3 (23)	K–Q3 (48)	30 P–B4 (18)	B × P (84)
26 K–K2 (137)	R–K1+ (31)		

CHESS 3.6 is now one Pawn up and also has a stronger position. COKO III is moving very quickly since there is little tactical play.

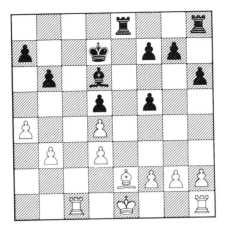

Fig. VII-10. *Position after 22 P–QN3.*

31 P–N4 (45)	P–KR4 (147)	34 K–K1 (56)	R–B7 (120)
32 B–K2 (26)	R–QB1 (124)	35 P–B5 (157)	R–R7 (98)
33 R–B1 (53)	B–K6 (53)		

Possibly less risky for CHESS 3.6 would have been 35 . . . , R–B8+; 36 B–Q1, P–N4, followed by an attack by the Black King on the White King's Bishop's Pawn.

36 P × P (40)	P × P (205)	39 K–Q1 (169)	R × P (95)
37 R–B6+ (49)	K–K4 (38)	40 P–N5 (87)	R–R8+ (264)
38 R × P (KN6) (41)	K–Q5 (276)		

(See Fig. VII-11.)

41 K–B2 (1)	R–K8 (124)	45 B × P (37)	R × P (64)
42 B–Q1 (53)	R–B8 (50)	46 B–B3 (41)	K–B4 (111)
43 P–R4 (176)	R–B7+ (63)	47 R–QB6+ (135)	K × P (46)
44 K–N3 (12)	R–B5 (48)	48 B × P (58)	R–Q5 (69)

COKO III must lose another Pawn, and CHESS 3.6 is well on the road to a victory.

49 B–B3 (57)	R × P+ (48)	51 K × R (2)	. . .
50 R–B3 (15)	R × R+ (18)		

(See Fig. VII-12.)

51 . . .   P–R4

CHESS 3.6 has the right idea, although it will occasionally get side-tracked.

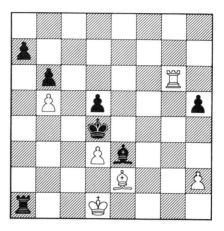

Fig. VII-11. *Position after 40 . . . R–R8+.*

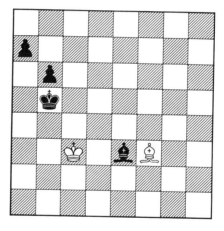

Fig. VII-12. *Position after 51 K × R.*

52 B–Q5 (12)	P–R5 (91)	58 K–K1 (32)	K–B3 (69)
53 K–Q3 (9)	K–B4 (144)	59 B–Q5 (24)	P–N5 (58)
54 B–K6 (39)	B–Q5 (148)	60 K–K2 (13)	P–N6 (41)
55 K–B2 (19)	P–N4 (52)	61 K–B3 (10)	P–N7 (75)
56 K–K2 (17)	K–Q3 (270)	62 B–K4 (17)	P–R6 (49)
57 B–B7 (14)	K–K4 (106)	63 B–N1 (20)	K–K4 (119)

(See Fig. VII-13.) COKO III can draw the game now! In the next three moves, it must move its King to QB2 and, after that, it must move its Bishop back and forth from N1 to R2 until the game becomes drawn by repetition. Any beginner playing White would realize that it is necessary

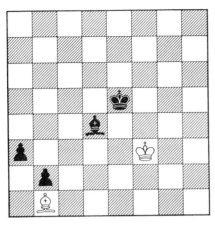

Fig. VII-13. *Position after 63 . . . , K–K4.*

to move the King towards the Pawns. However COKO III has no heuristics that encourage this. A twelve-ply search is necessary to see that Black's King can force a win by moving its King to QN6. COKO III is given the opportunity to draw the game for the next several moves.

| 64 B–R2 (12) | B–B6 (69) | 66 B–R2 (18) | B–N4 (96) |
| 65 B–N1 (20) | B–Q7 (97) | 67 B–N1 (31) | K–Q4 (129) |

COKO III is now finished. Its King is no longer able to reach QB2 in time; CHESS 3.6's King is moving in for the kill.

68 B–R2 (19)	K–Q5 (64)	71 K–Q1 (15)	P–R7 (19)
69 B–N1 (17)	K–B6 (77)	72 Resigns	
70 K–K2 (11)	K–N6 (33)		

Date: 8/14/72   Round: 2   Board: 2

WHITE: *TECH*   BLACK: *USC CP**

Sicilian Defense

1 P–K4 (1)	P–QB4	4 N × P (1)	N–B3
2 N–KB3 (1)	N–QB3	5 N–QB3 (1)	P–Q3
3 P–Q4 (1)	P × P	6 B–QB4 (120)	. . .

The first six moves by TECH repeat those played against CHESS 3.5 at the 1971 US Computer Chess Championship. TECH uses a very shallow tree search for these moves.

* Black did not provide a record of its time.

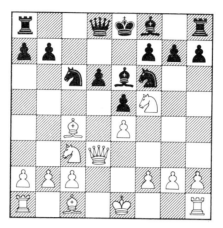

Fig. VII-14. *Position after 8 Q–Q3.*

6 . . .   P–K4   7 N–B5 (128)   B–K3

Black might have considered 7 . . . , P–KN3 followed by the fianchetto of its Bishop. Computers however rarely fianchetto Bishops, let alone plan it through a positional move such as 7 . . . , P–KN3.
  8 Q–Q3 (133)   . . .

(See Fig. VII-14.) TECH probably should have played 8 Q–K2 since 8 . . . , N–QN5 only forces its Queen to move again.

8 . . .	N–QN5	11 Q–K2 (148)	P–KN3
9 B–QN5+ (75)	B–Q2	12 B–N5 (139)	N–R4
10 B × B+ (109)	Q × B		

Black refuses to develop its Bishop.

| 13 P–QR3 (396) | P–KB3 | 15 N–Q5 (324) | Q–B3 |
| 14 P × N (191) | P × B | | |

Black cannot play 15 . . . , P × N because 16 Q × N+.

16 O–O (290)   . . .

More exciting might have been 16 P–N5, Q–B1, 17 P–N6, N–B5, 18 N–B7+, K–B2, 19 Q–N4.

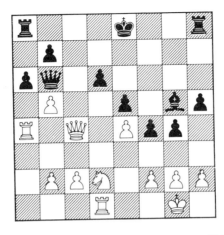

Fig. VII-15. *Position after 24 . . . , B–N4.*

16 . . .	N–B5	19 N–R4 (115)	B–K2
17 N × N (15)	P(N4) × N	20 N–B3 (57)	P–QR3
18 P–N5 (1)	Q–N3		

This is a rather weak move. Much better is a move that takes advantage of the open Queen's Bishop's file.

| 21 Q–B4 (158) | P–N4 | 23 N–Q2 (1) | P–KR4 |
| 22 R(B1)–Q1 (343) | P–N5 | 24 R–R4 (277) | B–N4 |

(See Fig. VII-15.) This move leads to Black's quick downfall. Much better seems to be 24 . . . , K–Q2 followed by 25 . . . , R(QR1)–QB1. White plays very strongly for the remainder of the game.

25 Q–K6+ (140)	K–Q1	29 Q × Q (96)	R–R3
26 N–B4 (239)	Q × P(N4)	30 Q–B5+ (61)	R–B3
27 Q × P(Q6)+ (90)	K–B1	31 Q–B8+ (1)	K–B2
28 N–N6+ (1)	Q × N	32 Q × R (849)	. . .

TECH takes almost 15 minutes for this. TECH was probably taking a good look at 32 Q–B7 and 32 Q–N7.

32 . . .	R × P	36 R–Q7 (820)	P–R4
33 Q–KN8 (49)	B–R5	37 Q–B7+ (85)	K–R2
34 R–B4+ (39)	R × R	38 Q × P(N7) mate	
35 Q × R+ (1)	K–N1		

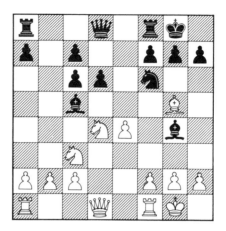

Fig. VII-16. *Position after 9 . . . , B–KN5.*

Date: 8/15/72   Round: 3   Board: 1*

WHITE: *CHESS 3.6*   BLACK: *TECH*

Ruy Lopez

1 P–K4 (B)	P–K4 (1)	4 O–O (B)	B–B4 (1)
2 N–KB3 (B)	N–QB3 (1)	5 N–B3 (104)	P–Q3 (1)
3 B–N5 (B)	N–B3 (1)	6 B × N+ (55)	. . .

CHESS 3.6 plays true to its reputation. It played from book for the first
four moves. TECH was using a shallow tree search.

6 . . .	P × B (99)	8 N × P (62)	O–O (27)
7 P–Q4 (79)	P × P (1)	9 B–N5 (109)	. . .

CHESS 3.6 was tempted to play 9 N × P, Q–K1; 10 N–Q5, but evidently
wanted to leave TECH's Pawns doubled.

9 . . .   B–KN5 (92)

(See Fig. VII-16.) Reshevsky observes that

> B–KN5 was amazing. But TECH had calculated that its move was not a
> blunder. It must have realized that if 10 B × N, Q × B, then: 11 Q × B,

* An analysis of this game by Samuel Reshevsky appears in *The New York Times,*
August 17, 1972.

B × N, with a playable game. And when White concluded it would not profit from the above continuation, it correctly played 10 Q–Q3.

It might be noted that CHESS 3.6 took longer to decide on this move than any other move of the game.

10 Q–Q3 (393)   B × N (124)   11 Q × B (86)   R–N1 (175)

This move allows CHESS 3.6 to weaken TECH's King-side Pawns. Reshevsky suggests 11 . . . , P–B4 and "if CHESS 3.6 persisted in its apparently intended continuation of 12 B × N, then 12 .. . , P × Q, 13 B × Q, P × N, 14 B × P, P × P, 15 R(R1)–N1, R(B1)–B1, 16 B × P, R × P, with an even position."

12 B × N (99)   Q × B (64)   14 P–QN3 (363)
13 Q × Q (46)   P × Q (105)

After only fourteen moves, the end game has been reached. CHESS 3.6 has managed to isolate two of TECH's Pawns while maintaining a good Pawn structure for itself.

14 . . .   R–N5 (50)   16 P–N4 (108)   R–Q5 (65)
15 P–KR3 (86)   B–K3 (45)

(See Fig. VII-17.) TECH is a little too passive about pushing its own Pawns. It might have played 16 . . . , P–Q4, encouraging an exchange of Pawns. The Rook move was motivated by TECH's desire to control and occupy central squares.

17 R(R1)–Q1 (182)   R × R (232)   18 N × R (28)   . . .

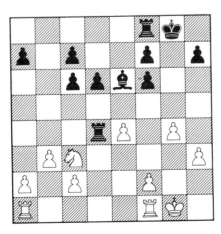

Fig. VII-17. *Position after 16 . . . , R–Q5.*

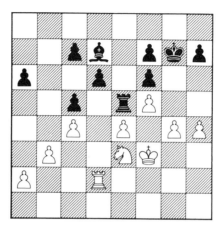

Fig. VII-18. *Position after 27 P–B4.*

Reshevsky notes that "CHESS 3.6 displayed good judgment . . . when it recaptured the Rook with its Knight instead of its own Rook realizing that the Knight could be better utilized at K3 than at QB3."

18 . . .	K–N2 (201)	20 P–KB4 (49)	K–N2 (206)
19 N–K3 (44)	K–N3 (242)		

This is necessary in order to avoid 21 P–B5+. CHESS 3.6 is gradually building up pressure on Black's King's side.

21 K–N2 (341)	R–QN1 (299)	25 R–B2 (88)	R–K4 (134)
22 K–B3 (120)	R–N4 (586)	26 R–Q2 (78)	P–QR3 (453)
23 P–B4 (55)	R–QR4 (317)	27 P–KR4 (126)	P–B4 (371)
24 P–KB5 (44)	B–Q2 (56)		

(See Fig. VII-18.) Reshevsky points out that this is an error and states that 27 . . . , P–R3 yields an even position.

28 N–Q5 (67)   . . .

Black is in serious trouble now!

28 . . .	B–B3 (12)	31 P × P (49)	P–R4 (178)
29 N × P(B7) (47)	B × P+ (42)	32 R × P (82)	B × P (271)
30 K–B4 (37)	P–KR4 (1)	33 P–R6+ (54)	. . .

Reshevsky gives CHESS 3.6 credit for a "stroke of genius."

33 . . .	K–N3 (1)	35 R × P (51)	. . .
34 P–R5+ (30)	K × P(R4) (47)		

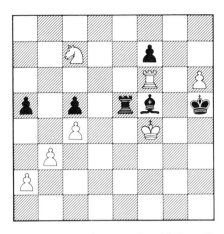

Fig. VII-19. *Position after 35 R × P.*

(See Fig. VII-19.) CHESS 3.6 has clinched the victory!

35 . . .	R–K7 (55)	44 R × P (61)	K–B2 (77)
36 K × B (22)	R–B7+ (1449)	45 R–R7+ (67)	K–N3 (305)
37 K–K5 (24)	R–KR7 (42)	46 P–R4 (148)	R–B4 (315)
38 N–Q5 (247)	K–N4 (86)	47 P–R5 (88)	R–B6 (54)
39 N–B3 (157)	R–R5 (104)	48 R–QN7 (102)	K–B4 (79)
40 R × P (61)	K × P (204)	49 N × P (50)	R–B6 (234)
41 N–K4 (82)	R–R4+ (122)	50 P–R6 (182)	R–R6 (1)
42 K–Q6 (54)	K–N3 (79)	51 P–R7 (61)	Time forfeit
43 R–QR7 (71)	P–R5 (178)		

Date: 8/15/72   Round: 3   Board: 3

WHITE: *SCHACH*   BLACK: *OSTRICH*

Nimzo-Indian Defense

1 P–Q4 (B)	N–KB3 (23)	3 N–QB3 (B)	B–N5 (56)
2 P–QB4 (B)	P–K3 (77)	4 Q–B2 (B)	O–O (60)

SCHACH has been using a book while OSTRICH has not. OSTRICH's authors felt that the book had not helped OSTRICH in the previous two rounds and thus decided not to use it for the last round. We were particularly unhappy with book lines when OSTRICH played Black.

5 P–K3 (133)	N–B3 (54)

White's 5 P–K3 is a bit passive; 5 P–K4 or 5 B–N5 or 5 N–B3 all seem to be stronger. OSTRICH did not play the usual 5 . . . , P–B4, 6 P × P, N–R3,

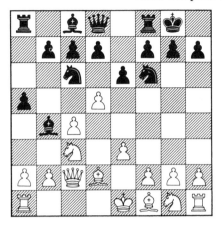

Fig. VII-20.   *Position after 7 P–Q5.*

recapturing the pawn on the seventh move because OSTRICH does not recognize that the sacrifice at ply 2 will be recovered at ply 5. OSTRICH stops search on this sequence after 4 ply.

6 B–Q2 (181)   P–QR4 (114)   7 P–Q5 (206)   . . .

(See Fig. VII-20.) This is SCHACH's first error and leads to the loss of a Pawn.

7 . . .	P × P (121)	11 B × N (150)	N × B (106)		
8 P × P (126)	B × N (104)	12 Q–B4 (173)	P–Q4 (151)		
9 B × B (172)	N × P (109)	13 Q–N3 (240)	B–B4 (244)		
10 O–O–O (248)	N(B3)–N5 (210)	14 P–QR3 (129)	. . .		

This is SCHACH's second costly error. Its Queen becomes trapped with

14 . . .	B–B7 (119)	19 K–N2 (151)	Q–N3+ (125)
15 Q–B3 (178)	N–R7+ (88)	20 K–R2 (183)	P–R5 (169)
16 K × B (85)	N × Q (42)	21 R–Q3 (224)	Q–N6+ (39)
17 P × N (125)	Q–N4 (141)	22 K–R1 (1)	Q × P(R6)+ (77)
18 P–KB4 (156)	Q–N3+ (67)	23 K–N1 (17)	R–R4 (60)

Black can hardly miss winning now. Even if it cannot find a mate, it can certainly push its Rook's Pawn and force a trade of a Rook for the Pawn. But White finds a move to help Black!

24 N–R3 (936)	R–N4+ (174)	26 Resigns
25 K–B2 (1)	Q–R7+ (211)	

(See Fig. VII-21.)

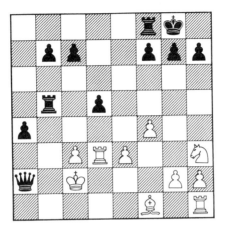

Fig. VII-21. *Position when White resigns.*

Date: 8/15/72 Play-off for second place Game 1

WHITE: *OSTRICH*   BLACK: *TECH*

English Opening

1 P–QB4 (B)	P–K4 (1)	5 B–N5 (B)	O–O (26)
2 N–QB3 (B)	N–KB3 (2)	6 N–B3 (213)	P–Q3 (1)
3 P–K4 (B)	N–B3 (1)	7 B–K2 (111)	B–K3 (77)
4 P–Q3 (B)	B–B4 (3)	8 O–O (103)	N–Q5 (1)

TECH has been playing with incredible speed. TECH uses a shallow search early in the game and thinks on its opponent's time.

9 N–Q5 (196)   P–B3 (1)   10 B × N (196)   . . .

Better for White is 10 N × N(B6)+, P × N; 11 B–R6, leaving Black with an isolated Pawn and somewhat on the defensive.

10 . . .	N × N+ (64)	12 N–B3 (97)	B–Q5 (101)
11 B × N (82)	P × B (1)		

TECH is in a strong position with control of the center. OSTRICH is most concerned now with avoiding the isolation of its Queen's Rook's Pawn.

13 Q–N3 (151)   . . .

(See Fig. VII-22.) This is quite weak. Much better are any of the following: 13 R(R1)–B1, 13 Q–B2, or 13 Q–Q2. Black is threatening to advance its Queen's Knight's Pawn to N4. White's Pawn on B4 is pinned, making White's position quite uncomfortable.

13 . . .   Q–R4 (171)   14 N–K2 (227)   . . .

Again, better would have been 14 R(R1)–B1.

14 . . .   R(R1)–N1 (157)   15 R(R1)–K1 (205)   . . .

OSTRICH does not use its Rooks well in closed positions. Either 15 N × B or 15 P–QR4 seems to give White a breather.

15 . . .   P–N4 (145)   17 Q–R3 (266)   . . .
16 N × B (229)   P × N (1)

OSTRICH is in serious trouble. For example, 17 . . . , Q × Q, 18 P × Q, P × P, and OSTRICH is in a real bind; if 19 P × P, then 19 . . . , B × P, winning for TECH at least a Pawn. If OSTRICH does not play 19 P × P, but tries R–QB1, it is still in serious trouble with 19 . . . , P–B6.

17 . . .   Q × Q (77)   19 R–B1 (117)   R–N4 (326)
18 P × Q (51)   P × P (1)

TECH's first weak move. OSTRICH has been given a reprieve. The reader might compare this move by TECH with move 14 in its game in Round 3 with CHESS 3.6. TECH wants to maintain strength in the center of the board. Much stronger was 19 . . . , P–B6, threatening B × P and R–N7.

20 P × P (111)   R–QB4 (454)

TECH's second weak move. Again 20 . . . , R–N7 was very strong.

21 R(KB1)–Q1 (134)   B × P (368)   23 R(B1)–Q1 (143) K–N2 (537)
22 R × P (97)   B–K3 (158)

TECH has given up its advantage. It seems to be a wide-open game at this point.

24 P–KR4 (256)   . . .

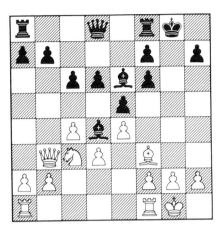

Fig. VII-22. *Position after 13 Q–N3.*

This allows White to defend its Pawn on QR2, to keep pressure on Black's Pawn on Q3, and to give its King an escape route.

24 . . .   R–B1 (730)

This move was motivated by the chess heuristic to place a Rook behind a passed Pawn. This heuristic haunts Black in the moves that follow. TECH took 12 minutes to decide on this weak move.

25 R × P (219)	B × P (265)	30 R–N3+ (93)	K–B1 (66)
26 P–R5 (91)	B–K3 (97)	31 P–R6 (185)	K–K2 (81)
27 R(Q1)–Q3 (114)	R–QN1 (97)	32 R–Q2 (71)	R–QB1 (76)
28 B–Q1 (123)	R–QB1 (159)	33 P–B5 (80)	B–B5 (71)
29 P–B4 (63)	R–K1 (189)	34 R–N7 (104)	. . .

OSTRICH could also have played 34 R–QB3, which leads to the win of the exchange.

34 . . .	R–K4 (78)	37 P–N3 (94)	R–KN1 (350)
35 R × P(R7) (170)	R × P(K5) (85)	38 R–N2 (174)	R–Q5 (602)
36 B–B2 (132)	R–R5 (61)	39 K–R2 (131)	Time forfeit

(See Fig. VII-23.) The position is quite complicated; it is hard to predict how this wild game would have finished if played out by the two computers.

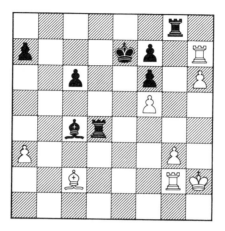

Fig. VII-23.   *Position at end of game.*

Date: 9/28/72   Play-off for second place   Game 2

WHITE: *TECH*   BLACK: *COKO III*

Petrov's Defense

Brace yourself for what follows! After a slugfest for the first 30 moves, TECH emerges with a passed pawn. Then for the next 100 moves TECH searches for a way to win while COKO III attempts to find a draw! TECH avoids a draw by repetition twelve times—on moves 41, 46, 50, 56, 64, 69, 77, 83, 99, 105, 110, 114, and 124! COKO III is given several other opportunities to draw the game—most dramatically when, on move 131, TECH plays P–N5—but loses the game with 135 K–Q1.

1 P–K4 (1)	P–K4 (100)	3 P–Q4 (1)	B–N5+ (381)
2 N–KB3 (1)	N–KB3 (142)		

This is the first of 70 checks—55 for COKO III and 15 for TECH!

4 B–Q2 (5)	B × B+ (85)	6 N × P (317)	O–O (200)
5 N(N1) × B (267)	P × P (311)	7 B–B4 (85)	N × P (273)

(See Fig. VII-24.) COKO III must have carried out at least a 5–ply analysis to see that 7 . . . , N × P; 8 N × N, P–Q4; 9 B × P, Q × P gives it a satisfactory position.

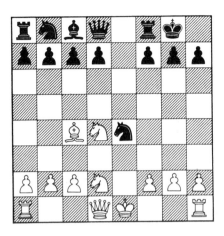

Fig. VII-24. *Position after 7 . . . , N × P.*

8 N × N (273)	P–Q4 (239)	12 N × N (296)	Q × N (116)
9 B × P (184)	Q × B (136)	13 N–N5 (291)	R–K1+ (391)
10 P–KB3 (248)	N–B3 (287)	14 K–B2 (280)	. . .
11 P–QB3 (305)	P–B4 (307)		

This move marks the first time in the nine games TECH has played in the US Computer Chess Championships that TECH has not managed to castle!

14 . . .	P–KR3 (308)	16 N × B (89)	R × N (165)
15 Q–N3+ (272)	B–K3 (118)	17 R(QR1)–Q1 (268)	Q–N3+ (70)

COKO III should have played 17 . . . , Q–B4+, followed by moving the Queen to either K4 or K6. White's next move 18 R–Q4 is a "natural" for TECH, increasing center control while defending the King.

18 R–Q4 (213)	P–B4 (208)	20 Q × Q (130)	P × Q (49)
19 R–Q5 (181)	P–B5+ (486)	21 P–QR4 (113)	. . .

(See Fig. VII-25.) This is a strange move for TECH to make. If TECH wishes to save its Pawn, why not 21 P–QR3. Otherwise why not play 21 R × P?

21 . . .	R × P (59)	27 P–B5 (211)	P × P (50)
22 R × P (82)	P–N3 (109)	28 R × P+ (128)	K–K3 (154)
23 R–Q5 (79)	R–R7 (72)	29 K–K4 (157)	R–R4 (199)
24 R–QN1 (108)	K–B2 (118)	30 P–KN4 (70)	P–R4 (165)
25 P–B4 (285)	R–K5 (177)	31 R × P (96)	R × R (169)
26 K–B3 (123)	R–K2 (171)	32 P × R (153)	K–Q3+ (83)

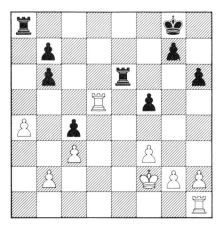

Fig. VII-25. *Position after 21 P–QR4.*

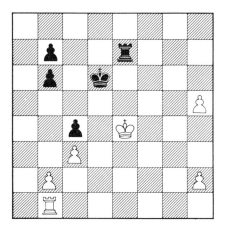

Fig. VII-26. *Position after 32 . . . , K–Q3+.*

(See Fig. VII-26.) Black should have played 32 . . . , R–R2, attacking the Pawn.

33 K–Q4 (140)	R–R2 (113)	38 K–K3 (108)	R–K4+ (50)
34 R–Q1 (109)	R × P (49)	39 K–Q4 (244)	R–Q4+ (36)
35 K × P+ (108)	K–B3 (42)	40 K–K3 (108)	R–K4+ (48)
36 R–Q2 (42)	P–N4+ (51)	41 K–B4 (49)	. . .
37 K–Q4 (199)	R–Q4+ (48)		

TECH avoids a draw for the first time.

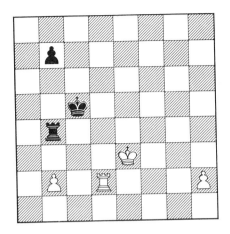

Fig. VII-27. *Position after 57 . . . , R × P.*

41 . . .	R–R4 (79)	44 K–K4 (70)	R–R5+ (52)
42 K–K4 (61)	R–R5+ (61)	45 K–K5 (253)	R–R4+ (35)
43 K–K5 (228)	R–R4+ (59)	46 K–K6 (129)	. . .

TECH avoids a draw for the second time!

46 . . .	R–R3+ (30)	49 K–K7 (165)	R–R2+ (45)
47 K–K7 (141)	R–R2+ (38)	50 K–B6 (247)	
48 K–K6 (331)	R–R3+ (37)		

TECH avoids a draw for the third time!

50 . . .	R–R3+ (48)	54 K–K5 (227)	R–R4+ (39)
51 K–B5 (64)	K–B4 (96)	55 K–K4 (228)	R–R5+ (46)
52 K–K5 (159)	R–R4+ (30)	56 K–K3 (67)	. . .
53 K–K4 (228)	R–R5+ (43)		

TECH avoids a draw for the fourth time!

56 . . .	P–N5 (69)	57 P × P+ (68)	R × P (62)

(See Fig. VII-27.)

58 R–QB2+ (335)	K–Q4 (49)	62 K–K1 (111)	K–K5 (56)
59 R–Q2+ (334)	K–K4 (55)	63 R–B4+ (107)	K–Q4 (39)
60 R–QB2 (337)	R–N6+ (56)	64 R–B7 (60)	. . .
61 K–K2 (88)	R–KR6 (77)		

COKO III can force a draw now. After the Pawn exchange 64 . . . , R × P;
65 R × P, if Black plays 65 . . . , K–B4, the game is drawn.

64 . . .	P–N4 (53)	67 R–Q7+ (133)	K–K5 (31)
65 R–Q7+ (58)	K–K5 (73)	68 R–K7+ (307)	K–Q5 (31)
66 R–K7+ (263)	K–Q5 (32)	69 R–K2 (48)	. . .

TECH avoids a draw for the fifth time!

69 . . .	P–N5 (120)	74 K–K1 (76)	R–R6 (36)
70 K–Q2 (489)	R–Q6+ (49)	75 K–Q2 (214)	R–Q6+ (35)
71 K–B2 (145)	P–N6+ (40)	76 K–K1 (76)	R–R6 (41)
72 K–B1 (95)	R–R6 (33)	77 K–Q1 (77)	. . .
73 K–Q2 (196)	R–Q6+ (35)		

TECH avoids a draw for the sixth time!

77 . . .	K–Q6 (44)	81 K–Q2 (152)	R–Q6+ (34)
78 R–KB2 (91)	K–Q5 (70)	82 K–K2 (150)	R–K6+ (33)
79 K–Q2 (415)	R–Q6+ (61)	83 K–Q1 (118)	. . .
80 K–K2 (157)	R–K6+ (36)		

TECH avoids a draw for the seventh time!

83 . . .	R–R6 (61)	87 K–Q2 (364)	R × P+ (54)
84 R–B4+ (37)	K–K4 (80)	88 K–B3 (242)	R–QB7+ (245)
85 R–QN4 (40)	R–Q6+ (49)	89 K × P (146)	. . .
86 K–K2 (91)	R–R6 (49)		

(See Fig. VII-28.)

89 . . .	R–B3 (54)	95 R–K4+ (218)	K–Q4 (34)
90 R–N4 (519)	R–QN3+ (80)	96 R–KB4 (219)	K–K4 (97)
91 K–B3 (124)	K–B4 (54)	97 R–K4+ (126)	K–Q4 (34)
92 R–Q4 (182)	K–K4 (81)	98 R–KB4 (247)	K–K4 (59)
93 P–N4 (211)	R–QB3+ (41)	99 K–K3 (37)	. . .
94 K–Q3 (159)	R–QN3 (47)		

TECH avoids a draw for the eighth time!

99 . . .	R–N4 (71)	103 K–K4 (145)	R–K4+ (30)
100 R–QB4 (228)	K–K3 (79)	104 K–Q4 (199)	R–Q4+ (74)
101 K–K4 (57)	R–K4+ (78)	105 K–K3 (118)	. . .
102 K–Q4 (205)	R–Q4+ (83)		

TECH avoids a draw for the ninth time!

105 . . .	K–Q3 (74)	108 K–K4 (159)	R–K4+ (185)
106 K–K4 (130)	R–K4+ (37)	109 K–Q4 (401)	R–Q4+ (35)
107 K–Q4 (167)	R–Q4+ (32)	110 K–K3 (99)	. . .

Fig. VII-28. *Position after 89 K × P.*

TECH avoids a draw for the tenth time!

110 . . .	K–K3 (80)	113 K–B4 (50)	R–KB4+ (34)
111 K–B4 (50)	R–KB4+ (38)	114 K–N4 (139)	. . .
112 K–K3 (64)	R–Q4 (57)		

TECH avoids a draw for the eleventh time!

114 . . .   R–Q4 (51)   115 R–B6+ (47)   K–K4 (53)

With TECH's King so far from its Pawn, COKO III should be able to find a draw.

116 K–B3 (351)	R–Q6+ (169)	121 R–B4 (115)	K–K4 (43)
117 K–K2 (287)	R–QN6 (52)	122 R–B4 (228)	K–Q4 (53)
118 R–B4 (370)	R–N7+ (50)	123 R–B4 (229)	K–K4 (81)
119 K–K3 (237)	R–N6+ (32)	124 R–N4 (227)	. . .
120 K–Q2 (239)	K–Q4 (59)		

TECH avoids a draw for the twelfth and last time!

124 . . .	R–N7+ (84)	128 R–K4 (119)	R–N6+ (42)
125 K–K3 (228)	R–N6+ (42)	129 K–B2 (159)	K × R (39)
126 K–K2 (197)	R–N7+ (52)	130 K × R (433)	K–Q5 (50)
127 K–Q3 (234)	K–B4 (60)	131 P–N5 (120)	. . .

(See Fig. VII-29.) COKO III can now draw the game and in fact has a drawn game for the next several moves.

131 . . .	K–B4 (40)	134 K–B5 (19)	K–B1 (66)
132 K–R4 (64)	K–N3 (30)	135 K–B6 (274)	K–Q1 (97)
133 K–N4 (9)	K–B2 (40)		

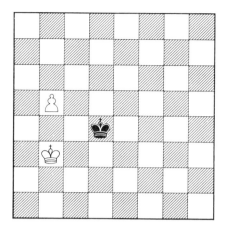

Fig. VII-29. *Position after 131 P–N5.*

TECH seems to know what it is doing. COKO III has just made the losing move!

136 K–N7 (460)	K–Q2 (39)	141 K–Q6 (132)	K–N3 (35)
137 P–N6 (361)	K–K2 (68)	142 K–K6 (78)	K–R3 (57)
138 K–B7 (123)	K–K1 (63)	143 K–B6 (83)	K–R2 (295)
139 P–N7 (264)	K–B2 (26)	144 Q–K8 (5)	K–R3 (1)
140 P–N8 = Q (79)	K–B3 (47)	145 Q–N6 mate (1)	

TECH, it might be noticed, maintained good control over its time during the course of this game. Gillogly had made several changes to ensure that TECH does not take too long on any particular move and consequently lose on time. In this game, TECH did not think on its opponent's time. The game lasted for about 10½ hours; TECH averaged 173 sec per move while COKO III averaged 84 sec.

Date: 8/18/72   Play-off for second place   Game 3

WHITE: *COKO III*   BLACK: *OSTRICH*

1 P–Q4 (14)	N–KB3 (24)	(1719)*	(569)**
2 N–KB3 (31)	P–Q4 (28)	(1908)	(592)
3 N–B3 (32)	N–B3 (56)	(3574)	(1255)
4 N–K5 (95)	. . .		

* This column is the number of terminal nodes scored. OSTRICH recorded this information as the game was being played.

** This column is the number of terminal nodes expanded (also recorded by OSTRICH while the game was in progress).

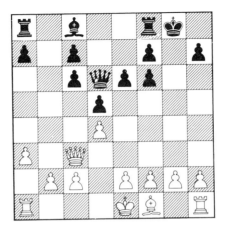

Fig. VII-30.   *Position after 10 . . . , Q–Q3.*

COKO III is looking for tactically oriented moves at a time when it should be looking for developing moves.

```
4 . . .            P–K3 (143)    (9024)    (3351)
5 N × N (38)       P × N (54)    (3284)    (1362)
```

OSTRICH is a little too willing to allow its Pawn structure to be weakened while COKO III is too willing to trade away a well-positioned Knight.

```
6 B–N5 (233)       B–N5 (98)     (5573)    (2952)
7 Q–Q2 (153)       O–O (157)     (9808)    (4085)
8 B × N (100)      P × B (82)    (4853)    (2110)
```

Better would have been 8 . . . , Q × B. Once again, COKO wastes a tempo and trades away a well-positioned Bishop, while OSTRICH allows its Pawn structure to be weakened.

```
9 P–QR3 (91)       B × N (85)    (5998)    (1911)
10 Q × B (51)      Q–Q3 (91)     (5848)    (2277)
```

(See Fig. VII-30.) This move defends the Pawn on QB3, prevents 11 Q–KN3+, and also threatens 11 P–K4.

```
11 Q–B3 (61)       . . .
```

COKO III is continuing to waste moves looking for tactical possibilities, while OSTRICH, with Pawn strength in the center of the board, is threatening to dominate that area.

11 . . .   P–K4 (139)   (10033)   (3219)
12 P × P (48)   . . .

COKO III remains consistent.

12 . . .   P × P (54)   (3710)   (1291)

OSTRICH has increased the fanout parameters at each level in the tree by one. So far OSTRICH has been averaging 84 sec per move and is ahead of schedule. OSTRICH will move faster than necessary throughout the remainder of the game, and consequently on every third move all fanout parameters will be increased by one until the fanout at ply 1 reaches the upper limit of 25. Presently the fanout parameters are 21, 23, 16, 12, 12, 12, with DMIN = 4, DMAX = 6, and AVEMT = 140. The gamma algorithm was implemented after this tournament (see Chapter X).

13 P–K4 (133)   P–KB4 (178)   (12587)   (4258)
14 P × P(B5) (221)   B × P (65)   (4687)   (1422)

COKO III falls a little further behind positionally. Throughout the tournament, OSTRICH has left its King with less protection than might be desirable. In this game also, the King is somewhat exposed but COKO III is not sufficiently well developed to take advantage of this weakness.

15 Q–KN3+ (401)   Q–N3 (100)   (7190)   (2095)

COKO III begins to play much slower at this point. Its fifteenth move took almost 7 minutes. This was the most time it spent on any move. OSTRICH's longest move is its sixteenth, which took just slightly over 4 minutes. White cannot play 16 Q × P because of 16 . . . , R(B1)–K1. It was expected that COKO III would play 16 Q × Q, but it chose to relieve an attack and to initiate a small attack of its own with

16 P–QB4 (326)   R(R1)–N1 (154)   (19700)   (6207)

(See Fig. VII-31.)

17 Q × P (271)   . . .

Disastrous! This move reflects a bug in the program's tactics. COKO III plays excellent chess for a program that has played only 20–30 complete games. The same type of error occurred in COKO III's game against CHESS 3.0 at the 1970 US Computer Chess Championship (see Chapter V, p. 61).

17 . . .   R(B1)–K1 (51)   (3627)   (1524)
18 Q × R (383)   Q × Q+ (24)   (1556)   (383)

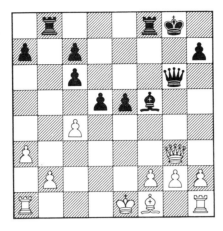

Fig. VII-31. *Position after 16 . . . , R(R1)–N1.*

It is only a matter of time now.

19	B–K2 (278)	R × P (147)	(11699)	(2129)
20	O–O (236)	Q × B (91)	(6161)	(3294)
21	P × P (126)	P × P (73)	(5025)	(2869)
22	P–KR4 (185)	. . .		

(See Fig. VII-32.) OSTRICH can win by simply trading material. However the bias for trading when ahead is not as large as it probably should be, and the reader can observe how OSTRICH, with a clear advantage, is in no hurry to trade material. However OSTRICH does like to push passed Pawns as we will see.

22	. . .	P–B4 (167)	(12204)	(5238)
23	R(R1)–K1 (266)	Q–R4 (128)	(9785)	(3875)
24	R–K3 (320)	Q × P (91)	(7070)	(2637)
25	R–K8+ (283)	K–B2 (82)	(6816)	(2092)
26	P–N3 (242)	Q–Q5 (131)	(10051)	(4333)
27	R–K3 (236)	P–B5 (114)	(8425)	(3787)
28	R–KB3 (393)	K–N3 (215)	(15885)	(7449)
29	R–B1 (332)	Q–Q7 (238)	(19001)	(7672)
30	R–R1 (215)	P–B6 (113)	(8244)	(4047)

OSTRICH predicts the sequence: 31 P–N4, B × P, 32 P–R4. It sees at this point that it can push the Bishop's Pawn to the eighth rank or force COKO III to give up considerable material to prevent it. Therefore it assumes COKO III will play like an ostrich, pushing the inevitable horrible con-

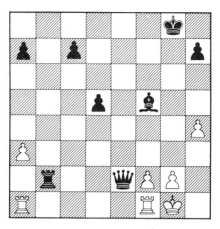

Fig. VII-32.   *Position after 22 P–KR4.*

sequences out of its mind by causing them to be too deep in the tree to be
seen.

31 R–B4 (199)	P–B7 (131)	(9021)	(5368)
32 K–N2 (189)	R–N8 (161)	(10686)	(6753)
33 R–R2 (224)	P–B8 = Q (84)	(5201)	(3916)
34 R–KR4 (198)	Q–N8+ (46)	(2440)	(2193)
35 K–B3 (84)	R–N6 mate (1)		

References

[1] Reinhold, Robert, In computer chess, blunders help, too, *The New York Times,*
August 17, p. 1 (1972)

[2] "CDC 6400 R-B4ch," *Newsweek,* August 28, p. 79 (1972).

[3] Reshevsky, Samuel, Analysis puts Fischer ahead of IBM, *The New York Times,*
August 17, p. 28 (1972).

[4] Newborn, M. M., A summary of the third United States computer chess championship, *SIGART Newsletter ACM,* 9–26, October (1972).

[5] ACM computer chess booklet, distributed at Ann. Conf. ACM, Boston, August
13–15, 1972. [Contains articles by authors of programs competing in the third
United States computer chess championship.]

[6] Samuel, A. L., Some studies in machine learning using the game of checkers,
IBM J. Res. Devel. 3, 210–229 (1959).

[7] Samuel, A. L., Machine learning, *Technol. Rev.,* 42–55, November (1959).

[8] Zobrist, Albert, and Carlson, Fredric, Jr., An advice-taking computer, *Scientific
American,* 93–103, June (1973).

[9] Mittman, Ben, Can a computer beat Bobby Fischer? *Datamation,* pp. 84–87,
June (1973).

CHAPTER VIII

KAISSA (1972)

A most interesting experiment took place in the Soviet Union in 1972
[1]. Beginning in 1971, Mikhail Domskoy and a group of assistants, working under Arlazarov, rewrote and improved the program that defeated
the Kotok–McCarthy CP in 1966–67. They named it KAISSA after the
mythological goddess of chess. Then in January, 1972, KAISSA accepted
a challenge. The Soviet newspaper *Komsomolskaia Pravda* invited KAIS-
SA to play a simultaneous two-game match against its readers; the newspaper would serve as middleman. On almost every Sunday throughout
the year, beginning January 15, 1972, *Komsomolskaia Pravda* published
KAISSA's move in each of the two games, and during the next few days
readers mailed in their replies. In each game the move fed into the computer was the move most frequently recommended by the readers. Several
thousand people participated in the experiment. Prizes were offered to the
100 readers who submitted moves that most often coincided with the
selected move. The final result: the readers 1.5, KAISSA 0.5. This result
is quite impressive; during the previous year Boris Spassky played *Komsomolskaia Pravda's* readers and only managed to obtain a 1.5–0.5 score.
One might conclude that the readers of *Komsomolskaia Pravda* are a
tough bunch and in turn that KAISSA can be no pushover either!

A listing of the two games is presented here. Scores given by KAISSA
to the positions were often published. Occasionally move times were
published along with the number of positions examined. The data indicate
that KAISSA evaluates about 12,000 terminal positions per minute. Search
was carried out to a depth of seven ply with captures and other forcing
sequences carried out many more ply. KAISSA used an ICL 4/70.

Game 1

WHITE: *KAISSA*   BLACK: *Readers*

1 P–K4 (+25)   P–QB4   2 N–QB3(+40)   . . .

KAISSA calculated for 40 minutes, examining 540,000 positions. It saw the six-ply principle continuation: 2 . . . , P–K3, 3 N–B3, P–Q4, 4 P–Q4, N–KB3.

2 . . .   N–QB3   4 B–N5 (+11)
3 N–B3 (+47)   P–Q3   . . .

631,000 positions were scored.

4 . . .   B–Q2   6 P–Q4 (+101)   P × P
5 O–O (+60)   P–KN3   7 B × N (+160)   . . .

The trap 7 . . . , P × N, 8 B × P, R–N1, 9 B–Q5, P × P, 10 B × P(N2), R × B, 11 Q–Q4 is beyond KAISSA's scope but was pointed out by the newspaper.

7 . . .   P × N   10 P–QN3 (+40)   N–B3
8 B × P   R–N1   11 B–K3 (+57)   . . .
9 B–Q5 (+12)   B–N2

1,500,000 positions were scored.

11 . . .   Q–B2   13 B–QB4   O–O
12 Q–Q4 (+85)   P–QR4   14 R(R1)–K1   . . .

A move quite similar in style to 15 R(R1)–K1 in OSTRICH versus TECH (1972). The move unnecessarily reduces the mobility of the King's Rook.

14 . . .   B–B3   15 P–K5 (−14)   B × N

The readers also liked 15 . . . , N–K1 and 15 . . . N–K5; 15 . . . , B × N was selected by a majority of 32 votes.

16 P × P (−25)   P × P   18 Q–Q3   B–K4
17 P × B   N–R4   19 B–Q4   K–N2

(See Fig. VIII-1.) Again the readers also liked 19 . . . , B × B, 19 . . . , B–B5, and 19 . . . , N–B5. The move 19 . . . , K–N2 received a 103-vote majority in anticipation of 20 . . . , P–B3.

20 R–K3 (+14)   . . .

KAISSA expects 20 . . . , P–B3, 21 B × P(B3), B × P+, 22 K × B, P–Q4+, 23 B–K5.

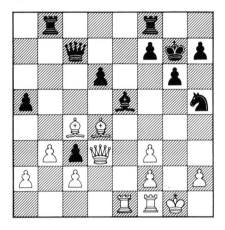

Fig. VIII-1. *Position after 19 . . . , K–N2.*

20 . . .	P–B3	25 K–R1 (+9)	Q–R6
21 R(B1)–K1	N–B5	26 R–KN1	N–Q4
22 Q × P (B3)	R(N1)–B1	27 Q × P(R5)	R–QB4
23 P–QR4 (+41)	Q–Q2	28 Q–R7+	R–QB2
24 B × B	P(B3) × B	29 Q–R5	. . .

KAISSA seems willing to settle for a draw.

29 . . .	R–QB4	33 R × P(K5)	R × P(B6)
30 Q–R7+	R–KB2	34 B × R	Q × B+
31 Q × R(B5) (−162)	P × Q	35 R–N2	
32 B × N	R–B5		

Declared drawn, Dec. 2, 1972. (See Fig. VIII-2.)

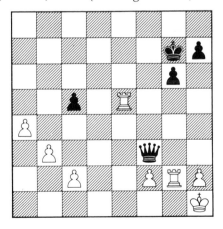

Fig. VIII-2. *Position at end of game.*

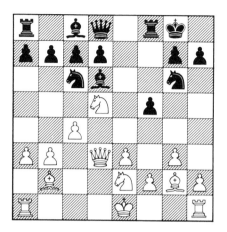

Fig. VIII-3.   *Position after 13 . . . , R–B1.*

Game 2

WHITE: *Readers*   BLACK: *KAISSA*

   1 P–QN3   P–K4 (+6)

White's first move was arbitrarily made before the readers were invited to participate. KAISSA required 10 minutes to examine 150,000 positions.

   2 B–N2   N–QB3 (+17)

KAISSA examined 1,500,000 positions in 90 minutes.

   3 P–QB4   P–B3 (+23)

KAISSA examined 720,000 positions in one hour.

   4 N–QB3   B–N5 (+49)   7 P–N3   O–O (+13)
   5 N–Q5   N(N1)–K2 (−12)   8 B–N2   N–N3
   6 P–QR3   B–Q3 (+101)

KAISSA examined 1,200,000 positions.

   9 P–K3   P–B4 (+3)   11 Q–B2   P–K5 (−28)
  10 N–K2   R–K1 (+9)

KAISSA examined 3,000,000 positions!

  12 P–Q3   P × P (−56)   13 Q × P   R–B1

(See Fig. VIII-3.)

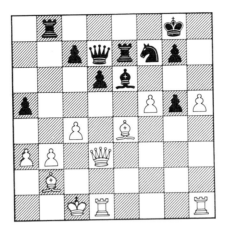

Fig. VIII-4. *Position after 30 . . . , N–B2.*

14 P–B4	B–K2 (−105)	16 P–R5	N–R1
15 P–KR4	P–KR3 (−139)	17 P–K4	P–Q3 (−171)

KAISSA examined 2,877,000 positions!

| 18 O–O–O | R–B2 | 19 N × B | Q × N |

White's move 19 N × B won by 27 votes.

20 N–B3	B–K3 (−143)	24 B × P (QN7)	R–N1 (−125)
21 N–Q5	Q–Q2	25 B–K4	N–B4 (−146)
22 N–K3	P × P (−138)	26 N–Q5	P–R4 (−139)
23 B × P (K4)	N–K2 (−116)		

This is rather weak! KAISSA has played several consecutive passive moves.

27 P–KN4	N–K2 (−115)	29 P–N5	P × P
28 N × N+	R × N	30 P–KB5	N–B2

(See Fig. VII-4.) KAISSA thought that 30 . . . , B–B2, 31 P–R6, P × P, 32 Q–QB3, R–K4, 33 Q × R would leave it in worse trouble.

31 P × B   Q × P (−113)

KAISSA predicts 32 R(Q1)–K1.

32 B–Q5	Q–K6+	34 R(Q1)–B1	Resigns
33 Q × Q	R × Q		

(See Fig. VIII-5.) KAISSA resigned on November 4, 1972, realizing that its position was hopeless.

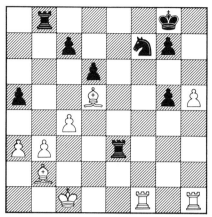

Fig. VIII-5. *Position when Black resigns.*

Reference

[1] *Komsomolskaia Pravda*, January 15, 23; February 5, 15, 19, 26; March 4, 12, 19, 25; April 2, 8, 15, 22, 30; May 13, 21, 27; June 3, 10, 24; July 2, 8, 15, 22, 30; August 5, 25; September 10, 17; October 17, 29; November 4; December 2.

CHAPTER IX

The Fourth United States Computer Chess
Championship (Atlanta, 1973)

The Hyatt-Regency Hotel in Atlanta, Georgia, served as the battlefield
for the most recent and best of the ACM tournaments. A record number of
entries led to an expanded field of twelve teams, which fought it out for
four rounds. The dates were August 26–28, 1973. David Levy served as
tournament director once again. After four rounds and several close calls,
the new program of Atkin, Gorlen, and Slate walked away with the championship for the fourth consecutive year.

Interest in computer chess continued to grow throughout the United
States in 1973; about twenty-five teams expressed an interest in participating in the Atlanta tournament. Based on the quality of sample games
submitted with their entry forms, what appeared to be the best twelve
teams were invited to play. This included seven new teams, three of
which seemed to have a chance to dethrone the program of Atkin, Gorlen,
and Slate. Alan Baisley, a researcher at the Artificial Intelligence Laboratory at MIT, had received permission from Jim Gillogly to participate in
the tournament with a modified version of TECH, called TECH II. Baisley
had added more positional factors to Gillogly's scoring function and had
improved the efficiency of Gillogly's move generators. Baisley indicated
that his program was at least on a par with Greenblatt's most recent version of Mac Hack Six. The Dartmouth University team of Warren Mont-
gomery and Larry Harris came well prepared with the Dartmouth Chess
Program. This program was written for the Dartmouth University time-
sharing system and had played hundreds of games against the local stu-

dent population. CHAOS, the work of Joe Winograd, Victor Berman, Ira Ruben, and Fred Swartz, was also expected to perform creditably. CHAOS searches a relatively small tree but spends much time at each node looking for good moves. The programmers developed their program at Sperry-UNIVAC and used a UNIVAC 1108 at Sperry-UNIVAC's Cinnaminson, New Jersey, plant.

The other four new programs were the work of Ken Thompson (T. Belle), a researcher at Bell Telephone Laboratories, Murray Hill, New Jersey; Charles A. Wilkes and Charles F. Wilkes (The Fox), a father–son team who used an IBM 370/145 at the College of William and Mary, Williamsburg, Virginia; David Barton, Craig Barnes, and Peter Rowe (CHES), who used a Hewlett Packard 3000 at the University of California, Berkeley; and Lawrence Futrell (the Georgia Tech CP), who used a Burroughs B-5500 on the Georgia Tech campus.

Five teams returned from the previous year. The defending champions had completely rewritten their program and renamed it CHESS 4.0. Using Shannon's type-A strategy and the old scoring function, new data structures permitted a search of 40,000 nodes per move. The OSTRICH returned, possibly somewhat the worse from a year of changes that were not sufficiently well studied. Many changes were made in OSTRICH and an insufficient number of games were played during the year to evaluate properly the effect of the changes. Some changes turned out well, others not so well. Gillogly returned with TECH, which had had its time control algorithms improved along with other only minor modifications. COKO IV represented the new work of Cooper and Kozdrowicki. It had several end-game algorithms added, which demonstrated themselves very satisfactorily in a victory over OSTRICH in the first round. The team of Zobrist, Carlson, and Kalme returned with the USC CP. They felt it had been improved from the previous year, although it still examined a relatively small tree.

The Tournament

Round 1 saw COKO IV avenge a defeat from the previous year by OSTRICH and saw TECH II lose its only game of the tournament—unfortunately on time while in a won position. CHESS 4.0 established itself as a strong defender of its title with a decisive 28-move win over T. Belle, while TECH, CHAOS, and the Dartmouth CP also won easily. The second round provided the biggest surprise of the tournament: after winning three ACM tournaments and ten consecutive tournament games, including a first-round victory in this tournament, CHESS 4.0 only managed to gain a draw in its game against the Dartmouth CP. Being in trouble most

TABLE IX-1

Final Standings of the Fourth United States Computer Chess Championship

Program, authors, computer, location of computer	Round 1	2	3	4	Points
1. CHESS 4.0; Larry Atkin, Keith Gorlen, David Slate; CDC 6400, Northwestern Univ.	W7	D5	W8	W3	3½
2. TECH II; Alan Baisley; PDP-10, MIT	L10	W12	W5	W9	3[a]
3. CHAOS; Ira Ruben, Fred Swartz, Joe Winograd, Victor Berman; UNIVAC 1108, Sperry-UNIVAC, Cinnaminson, N.J.	W12	W10	W6	L1	3
4. OSTRICH; George Arnold, Monty Newborn; Data General Supernova, Columbia Univ.	L8	W11	W10	W6	3
5. The Dartmouth CP; Warren Montgomery, Larry Harris; Honeywell 635, Dartmouth College	W9	D1	L2	D8	2
6. TECH; Jim Gillogly; PDP-10, Carnegie-Mellon Univ.	W11	W8	L5	L4	2
7. T. Belle; Ken Thompson; PDP 11/45, BTL, Murray Hill, N.J.	L1	D9	D12	W10	2
8. COKO IV; Dennis Cooper, Ed Kozdrowicki; UNIVAC 1108, BTL, Whippany, N.J.	W4	L6	L1	D5	1½
9. The Georgia Tech CP; Lawrence Futrell; Burroughs B-5500, Georgia Tech	L5	D7	W11	L2	1½
10. The Fox; Charles A. Wilkes, Charles F. Wilkes; IBM 370/145, College of William and Mary	W2	L3	L4	L7	1
11. The USC CP; Al Zobrist, Fredric Carlson, Charles Kalme; IBM 370/155, USC	L6	L4	L9	W12	1
12. CHES; David Barton, Craig Barnes, Peter Rowe; HP 3000, Univ. of California, Berkeley	L3	L2	D7	L11	½

Results of play-off for second place

	TECH II	CHAOS	OSTRICH	Points
TECH II	×	1	1	2
CHAOS	0	×	1	1
OSTRICH	0	0	×	0

[a] Won a three-way play-off for second place.

of the game, CHESS 4.0 seemed to be a certain loser; however, it fought gallantly and managed to gain a draw when the Dartmouth CP repeated a position for the third time. The Dartmouth CP was ahead a Pawn when the game ended, but it had no algorithm to prevent it from repeating a position for the third time when ahead! The Dartmouth CP drew with COKO IV while in a won position in the fourth round for the same reason.

In the third round TECH II defeated the Dartmouth CP, CHESS 4.0 defeated COKO IV, and CHAOS won its third straight game to take the lead in tournament. The fourth round pitted CHESS 4.0 against CHAOS; the winner would win the tournament (see Table IX-1 for final standings).

Both sides followed book openings for the first nine moves. CHESS 4.0 isolated a CHAOS Pawn on move 11, won it on move 15, won another on move 17, wrapped up the victory on move 23, and finally mated CHAOS on move 30. The game was a highly tactical one in which the large trees examined by CHESS 4.0 were too much for CHAOS to handle.

The tournament ended in a three-way tie for second place. TECH II, CHAOS, and OSTRICH all had three points. In the play-off, which took place during September, TECH II clearly proved its superiority, defeating both opponents easily, leaving in doubt how it would have fared against CHESS 4.0.

On the last evening of the tournament, after the CHESS 4.0 versus CHAOS game was completed, Charles Kalme played both programs in a simultaneous exhibition. Playing both games with a Queen handicap, he won the game against CHAOS (and a $100 side bet) but lost the game against CHESS 4.0.

Date: 8/26/73   Round: 2   Board: 1

WHITE: *Dartmouth CP*   BLACK: *CHESS 4.0*

Sicilian Defense

1 P–K4 (B)	P–QB4 (B)	4 N × P (B)	N–B3 (B)
2 N–KB3 (B)	N–QB3 (B)	5 N–QB3 (B)	P–Q3 (B)
3 P–Q4 (B)	P × P (B)	6 B–K3 (B)	N × N (54)

CHESS 4.0 finds a simple way to avoid isolating the Queen's Rook's Pawn.

7 B × N (116)   P–K4 (53)

The weak Queen's Pawn will give CHESS 4.0 a headache for the next sixteen moves.

8 B–K3 (110)   B–K2 (80)   10 Q–Q3 (1)   . . .
9 B–QN5+ (95)   B–Q2 (139)

This move was thought out on CHESS 4.0's time. The Dartmouth CP
thinks on its opponent's time.

10 . . .   O–O (40)   11 O–O–O (92)   . . .

The Dartmouth CP evidently wants to accomplish two things at once:
to castle and to put pressure on Black's Queen's Pawn. White might simply
have played 11 R–Q1 followed by castling to the King's side as soon as
convenient. White will soon forget that its Queen's-side Pawns are now
needed to defend the King.

11 . . .   N–N5 (86)

Black's Knight goes on a fishing expedition.

12 B × B (109)   . . .

A simplifying move is made. Other moves such as 12 P–B3 or 12 N–Q5
complicate the position and require at least a five-ply analysis.

12 . . .   Q × B (31)   13 N–Q5 (85)   B–R5 (32)

(See Fig. IX-1.)

14 P–KB3 (128)   . . .

Stronger was 14 P–KN3. If 14 . . . , N × B, then 15 Q × N and Black's
Bishop must retreat allowing White to advance its King-side Pawns.

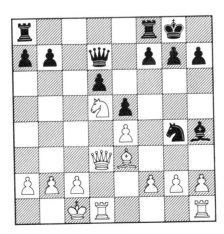

Fig. IX-1.   *Position after 13 . . . , B–R5.*

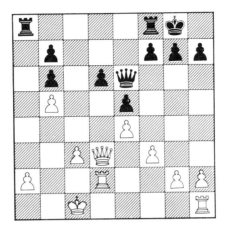

Fig. IX-2. *Position after 19 . . . , P × N.*

14 . . .   N–B7 (148)   16 R–Q2 (14)   . . .
15 B × N (1)   B × B (165)

The Bishop is harmless where it is and there should be no rush for White to chase it.

16 . . .   B–B4 (37)   17 P–QN4 (202)   B–Q5 (108)

Black is trying to avoid 17 . . . , B–N3, 18 N × B, P × N, 19 Q × P, because this leads to doubled Pawns.

18 P–B3 (166)   B–N3 (217)   20 P–N5 (1)   . . .
19 N × B (30)   P × N (83)

(See Fig. IX-2.)

White probably saw the four-ply sequence 20 Q × P, Q × Q, 21 R × Q, R × P, and was unimpressed. The five-ply sequence 20 Q × P, Q × Q, 21 R × Q, R × P, 22 R × P looks better but is, of course, refuted by the eight-ply sequence 20 Q × P, Q × Q, 21 R × Q, R × P, 22 R × P, R–R8+, 23 K–B2, R × R. Exactly what White saw in 20 P–N5 is quite unclear.

20 . . .   K–R1 (82)

This is a difficult position. But rather than 20 . . . , K–R1, Black should prepare an escape path for its King with 20 . . . , P–R3. Other possibilities are 20 . . . , R(B1)–B1 or 20 . . . , R(B1)–Q1.

21 Q–Q5 (147)   . . .

Both sides peck away at one another from now until the end of the game.

21 . . .	R(B1)–B1 (107)	24 K–R1 (147)	Q–B1 (128)
22 K–N2 (202)	R–B4 (127)	25 Q–Q3 (215)	R(N4)–R4 (76)
23 Q × P(Q6) (55)	R × P(N4)+ (74)	26 R–QN1 (156)	Q–B2 (74)

Black is forced to find squares on which to place its Queen that simultaneously defend all its weak Pawns and prevent a back-row mate.

27 R–N4 (152)	R–R6 (105)	30 R–N5 (52)	R(R6)–R5 (153)
28 R–B4 (54)	Q–K2 (109)	31 Q–Q5 (110)	Q–R5 (126)
29 R–N4 (48)	Q–B3 (115)		

A second fishing expedition is undertaken by Black.

| 32 R × P (196) | R(R5)–R4 (614) | 33 Q–Q6 (150) | . . . |

White's Queen must remain on the Queen's file to defend its Rook on Q2, but 33 Q–Q7 is stronger.

| 33 . . . | Q–K8+ (54) | 34 R–N1 (1) | Q–R5 (48) |

(See Fig. IX-3.) The Queen retreats to defend against the mate threat. Black evidently is not interested in a draw through 34 . . . , R × P+, 35 R × R, Q × P(B6)+, 36 R–N2, Q–K8+, etc.

35 Q–Q7 (82)	P–QN4 (120)	40 K–N2 (1)	R(B1)–R1 (82)
36 Q × P(B7) (206)	Q × P(R7) (61)	41 R–QR1 (40)	R(R4)–R3 (100)
37 Q–Q7 (1)	Q–B5 (107)	42 R–Q5 (126)	R–KN3 (71)
38 Q–Q8+ (140)	Q–B1 (59)	43 P–N4 (141)	R–KB3 (85)
39 Q × Q+ (1)	R × Q (1)	44 R × P(N5) (110)	. . .

Much better is 44 R–Q3, defending the King's Bishop's Pawn. White can simultaneously defend its own Pawns while attacking Black's isolated Pawns.

44 . . .	R × P(B6) (71)	47 K–N3 (82)	R(B6) × P+ (60)
45 R × P (97)	R–QN1+ (105)	48 K–N4 (110)	R–B7 (147)
46 K–B2 (197)	R–QB1 (94)	49 R–K7 (195)	R–QN7+ (159)

CHESS 4.0 attempts to force the White King to the side of the board in such situations.

50 K–R3 (1)	R–N7 (87)	54 R–R7 (28)	P–R4 (166)
51 P–K5 (114)	R × P(N5) (178)	55 P–R3 (213)	R–B5+ (134)
52 P–K6 (106)	R–N7 (212)	56 K–R5 (1)	R–B4+ (135)
53 K–R4 (212)	R–N7 (215)	57 K–R4 (135)	P–N4 (102)

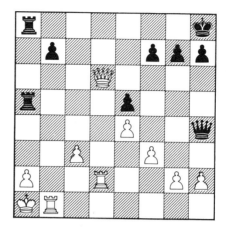

Fig. IX-3. *Position after 34 . . . , Q–R5.*

Black avoids a draw for the second time.

58 P–K7 (299)   R–B5+ (77)   59 K–R5 (1)   R–N1 (93)

Black avoids a draw for the third time.

60 R–K1 (257)   R–B4+ (106)   61 K–R4 (36)   R(B4)–B1 (116)

Black avoids a draw for the fourth time.

62 R–K5 (106)   R–R1 (59)   64 K–N5 (66)   R–K1 (284)
63 R × R (45)   R × R+ (85)

This move is forced. White can win with 65 K–B6!

65 R × P (115)   . . .

Two Pawns are better than one!

65 . . .   R × P (132)   66 R × P+ (29)   K–N2 (60)

(See Fig. IX-4.) White can still win simply by playing 67 R–KB5 and then advancing the Pawn [3].

67 K–N6 (26)   R–K3+ (249)   70 K–N5 (77)   R–K2 (77)
68 K–N5 (69)   R–K2 (77)   71 K–N6 (90)   Drawn by repetition
69 K–N6 (89)   R–K3+ (166)

CHESS 4.0 is willing to draw in this position. While unwilling to draw until now, its decision here was correct.

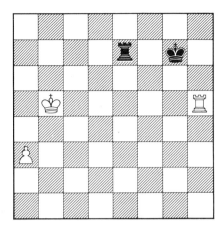

Fig. IX-4. *Position after 66 . . . , K–N2.*

Date: 8/27/73   Round: 3   Board: 3

WHITE: *TECH II*   BLACK: *DARTMOUTH CP*

1 P–K4 (1)	P–QB4 (B)	4 P–Q4 (234)	B–Q2 (102)
2 N–KB3 (1)	P–Q3 (B)	5 P × P (59)	P × P (118)
3 N–B3 (147)	P–K3 (122)	6 N–K5 (75)	. . .

TECH II is more aggressive than TECH. It combines the aggressiveness of Mac Hack Six with the thoroughness of TECH. TECH most likely would have developed a Bishop in this position.

| 6 . . . | Q–R5 (145) | 8 N–N5 (154) | . . . |
| 7 B–K3 (120) | N–KB3 (120) | | |

TECH II continues making aggressive moves.

| 8 . . . | N–R3 (172) | 9 N × B (259) | N × N (104) |

TECH II is concerned with saving its King's Pawn as the next few moves reveal.

| 10 Q–B3 (111) | N–K4 (166) | 12 B × Q (93) | . . . |
| 11 Q–B4 (43) | Q × Q (161) | | |

(See Fig. IX-5.)

| 12 . . . | N–KN5 (1) |

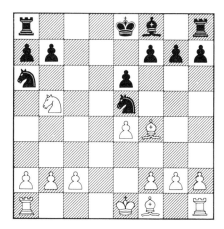

Fig. IX-5. *Position after 12 B × Q.*

Black's Knight is very weak on KN5. Better was 12 . . . , N–B3.

13 N–Q6+ (69)	B × N (69)	17 R(R1)–Q1 (145)	N–Q5 (74)
14 B × B (110)	N–N5 (26)	18 B × P (41)	P–K4 (180)
15 B–N5+ (38)	K–Q1 (105)	19 R–Q3 (83)	. . .
16 O–O (51)	N × P(QB7) (150)		

TECH II chooses to maintain the pin while centralizing the Rook.

19 . . .	P–QR3 (128)	21 B × N (59)	R × B (80)
20 B–B4 (52)	R–QB1 (124)		

Better was 21 . . . , P × B.

22 B × P+ (30)	K–B1 (104)	24 B–Q4 (114)	R–R5 (104)
23 B × P (94)	R–N1 (104)		

A move developing the King's Rook is much better—for example, 24 . . . , R–N3.

25 R–B1+ (42)	K–N1 (134)	26 P–KR3 (45)	. . .

Black is forced to pay for its weak 24th move.

26 . . .   R–Q1 (133)

(See Fig. IX-6.) Black will lose the exchange. In thirteen more moves, the Dartmouth CP will lose its only game of the tournament.

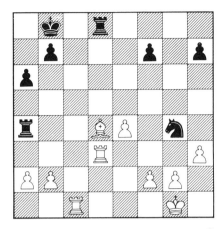

Fig. IX-6. *Position after 26 . . . , R–Q1.*

27 B–K5+ (88)	N × B (1)	34 K–B2 (23)	P–KB3 (171)
28 R × R+ (50)	K–R2 (1)	35 R–Q5+ (24)	K–B5 (1)
29 R–B3 (169)	R × P(R7) (116)	36 P–QN3+ (172)	K–B6 (1)
30 P–B4 (89)	N–B3 (142)	37 R–QB5+ (31)	K–Q6 (1)
31 R–Q7 (66)	K–N3 (46)	38 R × N (122)	R–R4 (1)
32 R–QN3+ (264)	K–B4 (177)	39 R–B4 (292)	. . .
33 R(N3) × P(37)	R–R8+ (167)		

TECH II took the most time on this move—almost 5 minutes. White has 34 legal moves in this position.

39 . . .   R–R8 (3)   40 R–Q7   mate

Date: 8/28/73   Round: 4   Board: 1

WHITE: *CHAOS*   BLACK: *CHESS 4.0*

Queen's Gambit Accepted

1 P–Q4 (B)	P–Q4 (B)	7 Q–K2 (B)	P–QN4 (B)
2 P–QB4 (B)	P × P (B)	8 B–N3 (B)	B–N2 (B)
3 N–KB3 (B)	N–KB3 (B)	9 N–QB3 (B)	N(N1)–Q2 (B)
4 P–K3 (B)	P–K3 (B)	10 B–Q2 (366)	B–Q3 (75)
5 B × P (B)	P–B4 (B)	11 R(B1)–K1 (341)	P × P (54)
6 O–O (B)	P–QR3 (B)	12 P × P (105)	. . .

(See Fig. IX-7.) CHESS 4.0 has managed to isolate a White Pawn.

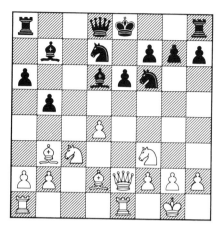

Fig. IX-7. *Position after 12 P × P.*

| 12 . . . | O–O (86) | 14 B–B2 (139) . . . |
| 13 B–N5 (269) | Q–N3 (108) | |

CHESS 4.0 now wins the isolated Pawn. White has 49 moves in this position. The book line results in a very complicated position. CHESS 4.0, searching a much larger tree than CHAOS, quickly gains the advantage.

14 . . .	B × N (48)	17 P–KN3 (177)	Q × P (105)
15 Q × B (142)	Q × P (209)	18 R–K2 (344)	. . .
16 R(R1)–Q1 (438)	Q–QN5 (226)		

Black must now defend against White's 19 B × P+. Thus,

| 18 . . . | Q–R6 (117) | 20 R × N (174) | R(R1)–B1 (174) |
| 19 Q–B6 (209) | B–N5 (176) | 21 R–B7 (102) | . . . |

White has 65 moves to choose from.

21 . . .	R × R (85)	24 B–Q1 (175)	R–Q1 (27)
22 Q × R (116)	Q × N (85)	25 R–K5 (70)	. . .
23 Q–N7 (299)	Q–B5 (56)		

(See Fig. IX-8.) White has made three consecutive weak moves while Black has pressed its advantage well. Black needs only six more moves to win the game and the tournament.

25 . . .	R × B+ (91)	28 K–K2 (111)	R–K8+ (121)
26 K–N2 (46)	Q–KB8+ (174)	29 K–Q3 (1)	Q–B8+ (114)
27 K–B3 (1)	Q–R8+ (106)	30 K–Q4 (5)	Q–B5 mate (1)

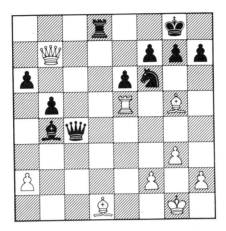

Fig. IX-8. *Position after 25 R–K5.*

The next game provides an excellent example of King–Pawn end-game play by computers. After 25 moves, only Pawns and Kings remain on the board. White has the advantage but does not know how to capitalize on it. Black, however, forces White to make the very moves it could not find on its own.

Date: 8/28/73   Round: 4   Board: 2

WHITE: *OSTRICH*   BLACK: *TECH*

Ruy Lopez

1 P–K4 (92)	P–K4 (1)	7 N × P (203)	B–K2 (312)
2 N–KB3 (92)	N–QB3 (1)	8 B–K3 (187)	O–O (308)
3 B–N5 (85)	N–B3 (1)	9 B × N (155)	B × B (107)
4 O–O (159)	N × P (1)	10 P–Q4 (113)	Q–B3 (304)
5 P–Q3 (119)	N–B4 (161)	11 P–QR3 (217)	. . .
6 B × N (125)	P(N2) × B (322)		

White neglects developing its Queen's Knight on this move and again on moves 13 and 16.

11 . . .	P–Q4 (219)	14 Q × R (1)	B–B4 (175)
12 R–K1 (203)	R–K1 (303)	15 Q–B3 (196)	R–K1 (292)
13 N × P(B6) (153)	R × R+ (101)		

TECH is quick to occupy open files for its Rooks and is now threatening mate.

16 P–KN4 (134)   . . .

(See Fig. IX-9.)

16 . . .   B–Q2 (127)

The position is quite complicated with threats and counterthreats by both sides. Black's best move is 16 . . . , B × P(N5), threatening 17 . . . , B–B6 or 17 . . . , R–K7, depending on White's seventeenth move. A thorough analysis of this position requires a deep search—deeper than that carried out by TECH.

17 P × B (111)   Q × Q (102)   18 N × Q (19)   . . .

Black forces White to develop the Knight!

18 . . .	B × N (198)	22 P–N4 (211)	R–B5 (294)
19 P–QR4 (43)	P–Q5 (83)	23 N × B (219)	R × N (140)
20 N–N5 (56)	R–K4 (294)	24 R–Q1 (214)	R–Q3 (263)
21 N × P(Q4) (224)	R × P (302)	25 R × R (51)	P × R (173)

OSTRICH's scoring function gives more credit for advancing Pawns than for centralizing the King. OSTRICH is also unable to see that the King should move in the direction of the advanced Queen-side Pawns. TECH will be seen to be equally unsure of how to proceed.

26 P–R4 (46)	P–Q4 (202)	29 P–KB4 (209)	K–B3 (50)
27 P–QB3 (64)	P–N3 (155)	30 K–B2 (208)	. . .
28 P–QR5 (49)	K–N2 (32)		

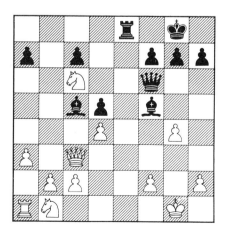

Fig. IX-9. *Position after 16 P–KN4.*

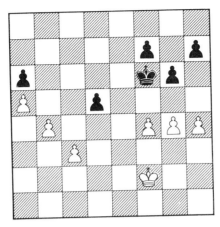

Fig. IX-10. *Position after 30 . . . , P–QR3.*

Black forces White to advance its King to save material.

30 . . .   P–QR3 (47)

(See Fig. IX-10.) In this position, White does not want to play 31 P–QN5 because this move results in a sacrifice at the second ply, the benefits of which are not felt for several more moves. The gamma algorithm (p. 177) stops search along this sequence of moves at the third ply, long before the Pawn reaches the eighth rank.

31 K–K3 (176)	K–K3 (124)	35 K–K3 (71)	K–K3 (181)
32 P–R5 (99)	P–B3 (114)	36 P–B5+ (128)	K–Q3 (200)
33 K–Q4 (93)	K–Q3 (146)	37 K–B3 (212)	P–Q5 (120)
34 P–R6 (39)	P–N4 (138)	38 P–B4 (77)	. . .

OSTRICH avoids the capture because it sees that the capture leads to the loss of its Queen-side Pawns: 38 P × P, K–Q4, 39 K–K3, K–B5, etc. OSTRICH does not realize that White will be able to queen a Pawn if the Black King tries to pick off these targets.

38 . . .   K–K4 (178)   39 P–N5   . . .

OSTRICH finally advances the Knight's Pawn—no longer afraid of an immediate loss of material, but still unaware that it can queen a Pawn. The queening of the Pawn is pushed beyond the end of the tree by the advancing Black's Queen's Pawn. OSTRICH saw the following principal variation: 39 P–N5, P × P, 40 P × P, P–Q6, 41 K–K3, P–Q7, 42 K × P, K–B5! OSTRICH has increased the depth of search so that for the last move DMIN = 6, DMAX = 8.

39 . . .	P × P (247)	46 Q–B6+ (139)	K–Q5 (199)
40 P × P (25)	P–Q6 (261)	47 P–N6 (149)	K–K4 (182)
41 P–R6 (143)	P–Q7 (66)	48 P–N7 (218)	K–B5 (209)
42 K–K2 (70)	P–Q8 = R (187)	49 P–N8 = Q+ (194)	K × P(N5) (200)
43 K × R (28)	K–K5 (106)	50 Q–K4+ (199)	K–R6 (2)
44 P–R7 (185)	K–Q4 (206)	51 Q–B3+ (164)	K–R5 (1)
45 P–R8 =	K–B4 (197)	52 Q (N8)–KN3	
Q+ (168)		mate (1)	

Date: 9/29/73   Play-off for second place   Game 3

WHITE: *CHAOS*   BLACK: *TECH II**

Queen's Gambit Accepted

1 P–Q4 (B)	P–Q4	5 P–K4 (338)	N–R4
2 P–QB4 (B)	P × P	6 N–K5 (216)	P–QN4
3 N–KB3 (B)	N–QB3	7 N × B (132)	. . .
4 N–B3 (B)	B–Q2		

CHAOS trades away a well-placed Knight rather than developing material. While CHAOS plays weakly for the next several moves, TECH II develops its pieces and clinches the game on move 12.

7 . . .	Q × N	10 Q–Q1 (273)	O–O–O
8 Q–R5 (227)	P–QB3	11 P–QN4 (145)	N–N2
9 B–K3 (186)	N–B3	12 P–QR4 (145)	P–K4

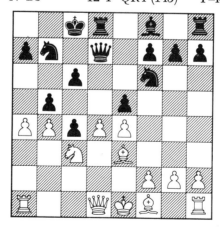

Fig. IX-11. *Position after 12 . . . , P–K4.*

* Black did not provide a record of its time.

(See Fig. IX-11.) White is in serious trouble now. Black wins a Bishop, a Knight, and two Pawns in return for a Rook.

13 P × P(K5) (109)	B × P	16 K × R (166)	N × P+
14 Q × Q+ (41)	R × Q	17 K–K3 (96)	B × N
15 B–Q2 (87)	R × B		

Although the game lasts another fifty moves, the verdict is never in doubt. Play is characterized by Black's attempts to pin or fork White's pieces. Material is gradually traded away; White finally succumbs on move 67.

18 R–Q1 (222)	N(N2)–B4	24 B × P (137)	R–N7+
19 P–B4 (331)	P × P	25 K–K3 (91)	P–R7
20 B × P (174)	R–B1	26 R–QR1 (353)	R × P
21 K–K2 (154)	P–R6	27 R × P (77)	R × R
22 P–N3 (119)	K–B2	28 B × R (193)	N × P
23 R(R1)–B1 (459)	R–QN1		

(See Fig. IX-12.) TECH II maintains its lead. Note how well TECH II controls the center.

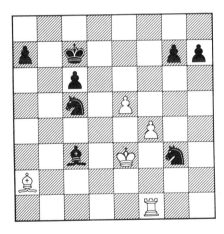

Fig. IX-12. *Position after 28 . . . , N × P.*

29 R–B1 (85)	N(N6)–K5	34 K–K2 (199)	N(B4)–K5
30 R–KR1 (137)	P–KR3	35 R–KN1 (177)	B–Q5
31 P–K6 (227)	K–Q3	36 R × P (120)	N–B6+
32 P–B5 (108)	K–K4	37 K–Q2 (101)	N × B
33 P–K7 (288)	N–Q3	38 R–N6 (105)	N–B6

39 R × P (217)	N(B6)–K5+	53 K–B4 (519)	N–Q4
40 K–Q3 (106)	N–B3	54 K–N5 (212)	P–R6
41 R–R8 (141)	P–B4	55 K–R4 (321)	B–B4
42 R–R8 (152)	P–B5+	56 R–KR2 (464)	P–B7
43 K–B2 (134)	K × P	57 R × P (390)	N–N3+
44 R–R8 (342)	K–K3	58 K--N3 (33)	N–Q5+
45 R–R4 (272)	N(Q3)–B4	59 K–B3 (119)	N–R5+
46 R–B4 (315)	P–R4	60 K–B4 (256)	N × R
47 K–N1 (261)	K–K4	61 K–N3 (192)	N–Q5+
48 R–N4 (253)	P–B6	62 K–B4 (231)	P–R7
49 R–N2 (343)	N × P	63 K–Q3 (1)	P–R8 = Q
50 K–B2 (325)	P–R5	64 K–K4 (45)	Q–KB8
51 R–K2+ (111)	K–Q3	65 K–K3 (1)	N–N6+
52 K–Q3 (187)	N–B3	66 K–K4 (1)	N–Q7 mate

References

[1] Mittman, Ben, and Newborn, Monty, Results of the fourth annual U.S. computer chess tournament, *SIGART Newsletter, ACM*, 36–48, October (1973).
[2] Kozdrowicki, Ed, and Cooper, Dennis, The Cooper–Koz chess program, *Commun. ACM*, 411–427, July 1973.
[3] Levinfish, Grigory, and Smyslov, Vasily, *"Rook Endings."* Batsford, London (1971). (First published in Russian in the USSR.)

CHAPTER X

OSTRICH: A Description of a Chess-Playing Program

A. Introduction

This chapter describes a chess-playing program written by George Arnold and the author and named OSTRICH because of its cowardly "head in the sand when in a crisis" style of play. The program was developed in the Digital Computer Laboratory of the Department of Electrical Engineering and Computer Science at Columbia University. Arnold was a junior in the department when the project began in June, 1971. During the fourteen-month period leading up to the ACM's Third United States Computer Chess Championship in August, 1972, we worked on the program approximately 30 hours per week; during the next year we invested about 10 hours per week. OSTRICH has played about 500 games against players of all levels—from beginners to Masters—including off-the-record games (all losses) with Masters Shelby Lyman, Rubin Fine, and David Levy. It also participated in a simultaneous exhibition against Grandmaster Walter Browne, losing in 50 moves. It has competed in one USCF rated tournament, although its rating is unknown at this time. Changes and improvements are continually being made; the version that participated in the ACM's Atlanta tournament is described in the rest of this chapter.

OSTRICH searches a large tree of variable-length move sequences using Shannon's type-B strategy supplemented by the alpha–beta algorithm. In turn, it supplements the alpha–beta algorithm with the *gamma algorithm*, which is discussed at the end of this chapter. Graduated forward pruning is performed at all nonterminal nodes. In the process of selecting a move, OSTRICH evaluates approximately 3500 terminal positions and 2000 nonterminal positions per minute.

B. Program Environment and Language

1. The Hardware

OSTRICH runs on a Data General Supernova computer, a minicomputer about the size of a suitcase, which sells for about $10,000. At present the program requires about 20K of core memory using about 9K for instructions and using the remainder for data, primarily lists generated during the tree search. The Supernova word size is 16 bits; instructions are of the single-address type. There are four special registers, two of which can be used for indexing. The Supernova executes memory reference instructions in 1.6 μsec and instructions involving only the four special registers in 0.8 μsec. Input/output instructions require somewhat more time. Thus the Supernova typically executes in the neighborhood of 900,000 instructions per second or slightly more than 100,000,000 instructions for a two-minute chess move!

Input/output for the Supernova is normally through an ASR 33 teletypewriter (10 characters per second). A 200-line-per-minute line printer is also connected to the Supernova and is primarily used for program listings and for observing the program in the process of searching a move tree. Additionally a 256K byte disk is used (1) to store source code, (2) to maintain a binary executable version of the chess program, and (3) to store a library of book openings. A miniature magnetic tape unit and a high-speed paper tape reader also serve as inputs. Permanent versions of the chess program are kept on magnetic tape and also on paper tape. A block diagram of the system is shown in Fig. X-1.

2. The Programming Language

When work first started on the program it was decided that the Supernova assembly language would be used rather than a higher-level language. While arguments can be made for using a high-level language such as FORTRAN IV, SNOBOL, LISP, etc., we have been quite happy working with the Supernova assembly language and feel that its selection was a good decision. Algorithms that are intended to improve the program's chess ability can often be added with minimal effect on the speed

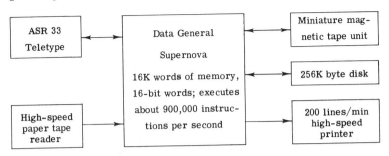

Fig. X-1. *System configuration.*

at which the program determines a move. Most modifications involve anywhere from 25 to 100 instructions and are written in several hours and debugged in several more hours. They are generally quite easy to make.

A single instruction in the Supernova assembly language can typically perform an arithmetic or logical operation using any two special registers, test the result, and conditionally skip—all in 0.8 μsec. For example: SUB 1, 2, SNR is an assembly language instruction that subtracts the contents of special register 1 from special register 2, leaving the difference in special register 2 and then skipping the next instruction if the result of the subtraction is not zero. This type of instruction is quite advantageous since a chess program contains a large number of conditional branches. The searching of lists is accomplished relatively easily on the Supernova by using special memory locations that serve as autoincrementing or autodecrementing registers. There are eight of each type.

C. Program Organization and Data Structures

1. The Three Programs

OSTRICH consists of three separate programs: a BOOK program, a main CHESS playing program, and a special END GAME program (Fig. X-2). During a game, only one of the three programs is in core memory at a time while the other two are stored on disk. A game begins with OSTRICH using either the BOOK program or the main CHESS program. BOOK has about 400 opening lines with no more than five full moves in any line; this restricts the use of BOOK to at most the first five moves. The choice of whether to begin with BOOK or CHESS is made

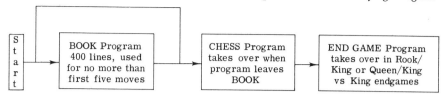

Fig. X-2.   *Program   organization.*

by the human operator in charge of the computer. BOOK serves two functions: (1) it provides good moves and (2) it provides them quickly, thus allowing more time for other moves. The openings were selected based on their suitability for the style of play exhibited by OSTRICH. OSTRICH is uncomfortable with certain openings, and an attempt was made to avoid them, as was discussed when Berliner's program was described in Chapter IV.

Most of a game is played in the main program simply called CHESS. With the exception of the remainder of this paragraph, we will be concerned with the CHESS program of OSTRICH, although we will call it OSTRICH rather than CHESS. If OSTRICH ever finds itself in an end-game situation in which it has only a Queen or Rook and King against its opponent's lone King, a special END GAME program takes control and forces checkmate. The END GAME program does not search a tree of moves; each move is selected based on an algorithm that mates the lone King with a Rook and a King. If a Queen is on the board instead of a Rook, the Queen is treated as though it were a Rook.

2.   The Main Program—CHESS

The approximately 9000 instructions of CHESS are functionally divided into five segments or subprograms.

(1) A segment for input/output and user communication and for tree-size control. This segment is in control when a move is being entered into the Supernova or when the Supernova is printing out its move, etc. The tree-size control part of this segment controls the size of the tree that the Supernova examines on each move.

(2) A move and tree generator segment. This segment is in control when the moves lists are being generated and the tree is being searched.

(3) A segment devoted to ordering the moves list for each nonterminal position in order to maximize the number of cutoffs that occur. Once the moves have been generated at a nonterminal position in the tree, this segment assigns a *plausibility score* to each of the moves and then orders them on a moves list according to their score, the move with the

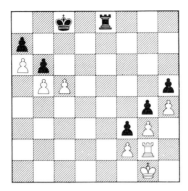

(a)

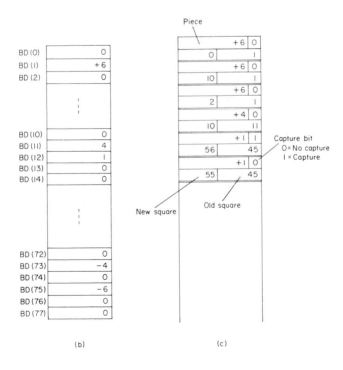

(b)   (c)

Fig. X-3. *A board (a) with corresponding board position list (b) and moves list at ply 1 (c).*

highest score being placed at the top. After this initial ordering has been completed, several special reordering routines are called upon. These routines attempt to improve on the initial ordering.

(4) A segment devoted to calculating the *terminal score* of each terminal position. The terminal scoring function is called upon to evaluate the board at each terminal position in the tree.

(5) A segment that updates the various lists and pointers used by the rest of the program.

3.   Data Structures of CHESS

The major lists that the program makes use of are:

(1) *The board position list.*   The board position list is stored in 64 consecutive memory locations. The board position list is continually updated and restored as the tree search is carried out. Each piece is represented by an integer: White King is +6, White Queen +5, White Rook +4, White Bishop +3, White Knight +2, and White Pawn +1. An empty square is 0; a black piece is represented by the negative of the integer used to represent the corresponding white piece.

(2) *The piece location list.*   This list is generated at the beginning of the tree search. Two separate lists actually exist— one for White and one for Black. This list is continually updated and restored as the tree search progresses. The size is 64 words—32 words to represent the pieces and 32 words to denote their squares.

(3) *A moves list.*   With the exception of a terminal position, for every board position on the continuation of the tree undergoing analysis, there is a corresponding *moves list*. These lists are stored contiguously in memory with the list for ply 2 immediately following the list for ply 1, the list for ply 3 immediately following the list for ply 2, etc. Each move is stored in two consecutive memory words. The piece and whether or not the move is a capture are stored in one word and the old and new squares are stored in the second word. This is shown in Fig. X-3. About 1000 words of memory space are reserved to store this information.

(4) *A control list.*   This list indicates the squares controlled by each piece. It is possible to reference this list either by the square of the controlling piece or by the controlled square. Thus, for example, it is equally easy to obtain from this list either all of the squares that a particular piece controls (directly or indirectly through, say, a screened attack) or the squares of all pieces that control a given square. This list is continually updated and restored. About 1000 words of memory are used for this list.

(5) *A change list.* This list records the changes that are made at a node in the tree when advancing to a new node. By using this list, restoring positions can be carried out considerably faster than updating positions. Again, this list occupies about 1000 memory locations.

The program generates and makes use of numerous other smaller lists, none of which contains more than about one hundred elements. Among these are:

(6) *A pinned piece list.* There is a separate list of pinned pieces for each node on the continuation currently being investigated.

(7) *An en prise piece list.* Similarly, there is a separate list for each node on the continuation under study.

(8) *Alpha and beta refutation moves lists.* A list is kept of the eight most recent moves that caused alpha-cutoffs. Another is kept of the eight most recent moves that caused beta-cutoffs.

(9) *A third-ply best-response list.* As the tree is being searched, OSTRICH generates a list of the best third-ply move to each second-ply opponent's move to, in turn, each move investigated by OSTRICH at ply 1. This list often gives OSTRICH a good move to put at the top of the ply-1 moves list on the next move.

(10) *A principal variation list.* A list containing the principal variation found thus far in the tree search.

(11) *A past positions list.* A list containing all past positions since the last capture or Pawn move. This list is used to detect draws by repetition.

D. The Tree Size

1. Tree-Size Parameters

At the beginning of a game (or, in fact, before every move) there are various parameters that can be set or adjusted which determine the size of the tree. The size is, in turn, closely related to the amount of time a move calculation requires.

(1) *Fanout parameters* (F1, F2, . . . , F10). The fanout at all levels beyond ply 10 is automatically set to F10. The fanout at each level in the tree can be arbitrarily set to any positive integer.

(2) *Search depth parameters* (DMIN, DMAX). The depth to which sequences of moves are examined is determined primarily by DMIN and DMAX. Positions at a depth less than DMIN are considered

nonterminal positions unless the gamma algorithm specifies otherwise. (The gamma algorithm is described at the end of this chapter.) Positions at a depth greater than DMIN and less than DMAX are considered terminal positions if (1) the gamma algorithm specifies that they are or (2) certain features are not present that specify a deeper search be carried out. These features are checks, captures, Pawn promotions at the previous ply, the presence of en prise pieces, or Pawns on the seventh rank. In these cases, search is extended one ply at a time to a depth of DMAX. All positions examined at depth DMAX are automatically considered terminal positions and scored.

(3) *Average move time* (AVEMT).   The rate (in seconds) at which one wishes the computer to make its moves can be arbitrarily set to any positive integer. Most frequently the authors have used 90 sec as a default value for AVEMT.

(4) *Total time* (TOTTM).   The total amount of time the computer has consumed so far to make all its moves is accumulated in TOTTM. Book moves are made in zero time. After each move the computer updates TOTTM.

(5) *Artificial time* (ARTTM).   The value of ARTTM equals the number of (nonbook) moves multiplied by the AVEMT. If on some move the ARTTM is less than the TOTTM, then the computer is "behind schedule."

For tournament-level play (40 moves in 2 hours and then 10 moves every 30 minutes thereafter) the parameters are typically initialized to the following values: F1 = 21, F2 = 25, F3 = 16, F4 = 16, F5 = 10, F6 = 9, F7 = 9, F8 = 9, F9 = 9, F10 = 9, DMIN = 5, DMAX = 7, AVEMT = 137 sec. If the gamma algorithm is removed from the program, DMIN = 4, DMAX = 6.

2.   Control of Tree Size

During the course of a game, if the parameters F1, F2, . . . , F10, DMIN, and DMAX are left at their initial values, one would find considerable variation in the amount of time OSTRICH requires to decide each move. Most notably, as OSTRICH reaches end-game positions, a large speedup would be observed in the rate at which moves are determined. Also, upon the disappearance of the two Queens, a marked speedup would be noticed. On the other hand, when OSTRICH is in a bad position or when no move appears particularly good, moves are decided more slowly. Thus to ensure that OSTRICH takes advantage of all its allotted time and alternatively to ensure that it does not fall into time pressure, the parameters F1, F2, . . . , F10, DMIN, DMAX, and AVEMT are adjusted before each move, as follows:

(1) For each move that OSTRICH selects from BOOK for itself, it increases AVEMT by 2 sec. When the fortieth move is reached, AVEMT is automatically restored to its original value.

(2) Starting on the twelfth move and on every move thereafter, OSTRICH considers whether to reduce its fanout parameters. Each fanout parameter is reduced by 1 if the ARTTM is less than the TOTTM, that is, if moves are being made too slowly.

(3) Starting on the twelfth move and on every third move thereafter OSTRICH considers whether to increase its fanout parameters. Each fanout parameter is increased by 1 if the ARTTM is greater than the TOTTM, that is, if moves are being made faster than necessary.

(4) DMIN and DMAX are both increased by 1 whenever the total time required to make three consecutive moves is less than $1.5 \times$ AVEMT. Quite often DMIN and DMAX are extended to values of 6 and 8, respectively, in end-game play. In very late end-game play, with only about 10 moves per side in a given position, DMIN and DMAX can be increased to values of 7 and 9 and occasionally to values of 8 and 10, while still allowing OSTRICH to make moves fast enough for tournament play.

(5) DMIN and DMAX are reduced by 1 during the course of any move calculation whenever the amount of time spent on that particular move exceeds $1.5 \times$ AVEMT. This helps to ensure that no single move takes an excessive amount of time. At the start of the next move, DMIN and DMAX assume the values they had at the start of the previous move.

(6) DMIN and DMAX are reduced by 1 at the beginning of a move if TOTTM > ARTTM; i.e., if OSTRICH is behind schedule, DMIN and DMAX are reduced.

(7) The values of DMIN, DMAX, F1, F2, . . . , F10 have lower bounds that can be entered into the computer at the beginning of play; these can also be changed at the beginning of any move. During the course of a game, if the lower bounds are reached, OSTRICH will not reduce DMIN, DMAX, F1, F2, . . . , F10 any further even if the program is in time trouble. For most play the lower bounds on DMIN and DMAX are 5 and 7, respectively.

E. Processing at Each Node

Figure X-4 is a flow chart broadly outlining the processing that occurs when a new node is reached. Processing begins with several tests

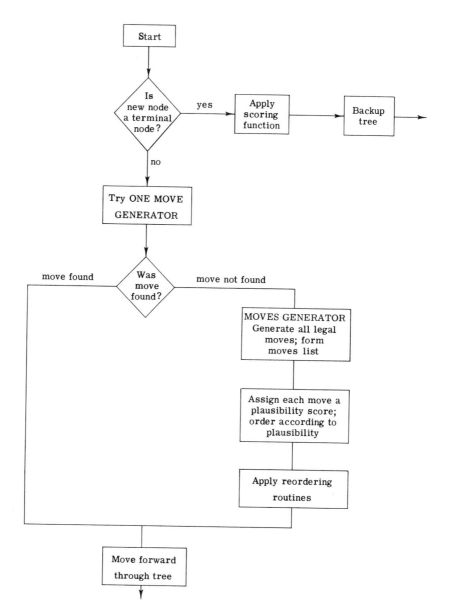

Fig. X-4.   *General flow chart of processing at a node.*

that determine whether the node should be considered a *terminal node* or a *nonterminal node*. A node is a terminal node if

(1) it is at ply DMAX,
(2) it is at ply DMIN or greater, and there are no special features on the board (see p. 164), or
(3) it is specified as being so by the gamma algorithm.

Otherwise a node is a nonterminal node. Processing a nonterminal node averages about 49 msec while a terminal node requires about 10 msec.

F.   Nonterminal Node Processing

1.   One Move Generator

Processing at each new nonterminal node begins with the ONE MOVE GENERATOR. It checks whether all legal moves must be generated or whether one may be sufficient. For example, at the time when processing begins at node N_a in the tree in Fig. X-5, it can be determined that none of the moves M_{a_1}, M_{a_2}, . . . , M_{a_n} will cause a cutoff. At node N_b, however, this is not the case; the *first move* processed at node N_b *could* refute move M_2. If OSTRICH decides that the first move processed could cause a refutation, it continues with the ONE MOVE GENERATOR; otherwise, it jumps to the MOVES GENERATOR.

The ONE MOVE GENERATOR checks whether moves that have previously been found to be "good" in other positions can also be made

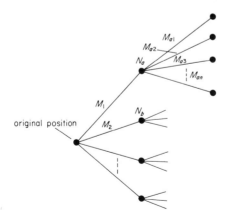

Fig. X-5.   *A tree illustrating one-move generation.*

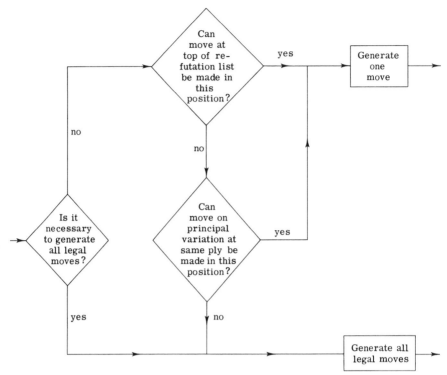

Fig. X-6. *Decision process for move generation.*

in this position. It first checks whether the last refutation can be made.
If so, it is selected for the good move. If not, it next checks whether the
move on the principal variation at the same ply can be made. If so, it
selects this move for the good move. If not, processing jumps to the
MOVES GENERATOR. This is shown in the flow chart in Fig. X-6. The
reader should note that the ONE MOVE GENERATOR might select
a move that turns out to be weak and that does not cause a cutoff. In
this case, when processing returns to this node, OSTRICH jumps directly
to the MOVES GENERATOR. It has been our experience that the moves
selected by the ONE MOVE GENERATOR cause cutoffs at 40–50% of
the nodes in the tree!

2.   Move Generation, Plausibility Analysis, and Reordering Routines

The MOVES GENERATOR generates the moves list, a list of all
legal moves—illegal moves are never put on the list. If a move has been
previously selected by the ONE MOVE GENERATOR, it is weeded out

from this list. Moves are generated for each piece on the piece list by a PAWN MOVE GENERATOR, KNIGHT MOVE GENERATOR, etc., and are placed on the moves list. Once the moves list has been generated, each move is assigned a plausibility score and then the entire list is ordered in descending order of plausibility. Finally several special reordering routines reorder the list.

Plausibility Analysis

Each move is assigned a score by the plausibility analysis subroutine, as indicated in the flow chart in Fig. X-7. The factors used to determine the plausibility of a move vary from piece to piece and depend also on the stage of the game.

Captures. A capture receives a score of 2400° points plus a factor that depends on the relative values of the pieces involved in the capture as indicated by the following formula:

$$\text{capture points} = 2400 + (\text{value of captured piece} - \text{value of capturing piece})/10$$

where the values of the pieces are as follows: Pawn = 600 points, Knight = Bishop = 3 Pawns, Rook = 5 Pawns, Q = 9 Pawns, and K = 500 Pawns. If a move is found to be a capture, no further plausibility analysis is carried out on it.

Castling. A castling move is given a plausibility score of 10,000 points. This ensures that a castling move is placed at the top of a moves list. If a move is found to be a castling move, no further plausibility analysis is carried out on it.

The Mixer. This factor effectively adds a random number of points (somewhere from 0 to 10) to all moves except captures and castling moves. This factor was added early in the development of the program; it helps to ensure that no piece has an excessive number of moves on the moves list while another has too few. As the plausibility analysis has become more refined, this factor has become less important.

Advance. A penalty is given to any move that retreats a Knight, Bishop, or Queen (−20 points). This factor encourages examining moves that advance one of these pieces.

Immediate Pawn Attack. A penalty of 200 points is given to a move

---

° Note: All numbers in this section and in the section describing the scoring function are octal numbers.

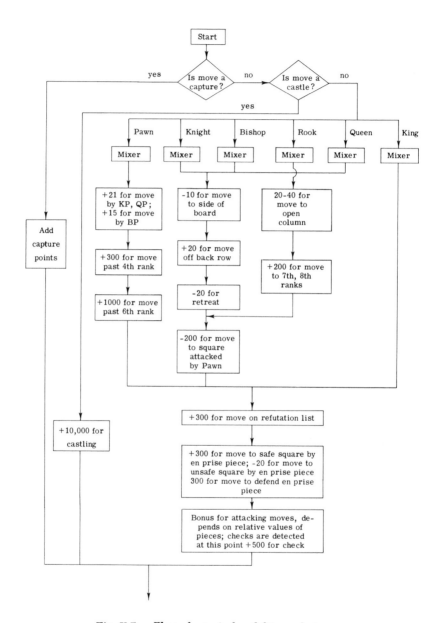

Fig. X-7. *Flow chart of plausibility analysis.*

by a Queen, Rook, Bishop, or Knight to a square where it can be immediately captured by a Pawn.

Special Pawn Scoring. (a) A move by a King's Pawn or Queen's Pawn is given 21 extra points; a move by a Bishop's Pawn is given 15 points. (b) A Pawn move past the fourth rank is given 300 extra points. (c) A Pawn move to the seventh or eighth ranks is given 1000 extra points.

Special Knight, Bishop, and Queen Scoring. (a) A move off the first rank is given a 20-point bonus. (b) A move to a side column is given a 10-point penalty.

Special Rook Scoring. Rooks are encouraged to move to columns in which there are no Pawns. In particular, a move by a Rook on rank 1 to a square also on rank 1 that has no Pawns on ranks 2 and 3 is given a 20-point bonus; no Pawns on ranks 2–4 implies a 40-point bonus. Rooks are also encouraged to move to the seventh and eighth ranks (+200-point bonus).

Refutation Moves Scoring. Lists are kept of moves that cause cutoffs in the alpha–beta algorithm, one list for alpha-cutoffs and one list for beta-cutoffs. The list that stores alpha-cutoffs is a pushdown list that keeps track of the eight most recent moves that caused alpha-cutoffs; similarly, the list that stores beta-cutoffs is organized in the same way. These lists are constantly being updated during the tree search. If a move is found to be on the appropriate refutation list it is given 300 points.

En Prise Bonus. If a piece is en prise on its present square, a check is made of squares to which it can move. A move to a safe square is given 300 points credit while a move to an unsafe square receives a 20-point penalty. A move that defends an en prise piece is given a 300-point bonus.

Attacking Moves. A move that takes a piece to a square on which it is attacking more pieces than it previously attacked receives credit according to a relatively complex formula. Checks are picked up in this algorithm and are given a 500-point bonus.

Reordering Routines

As work on the program progressed it became apparent that the number of cutoffs could be increased if several reordering routines were performed after the moves had been ordered according to their plausibility score. When the plausibility analysis has been completed, castling moves are at the top of the moves list and captures are placed next, followed by the rest of the moves.

Capture Reordering. Since a capture is usually not the best move in most positions, it pays not to place them at the top of a moves list quite as arbitrarily as is done by the plausibility analysis. This is especially true at early plies in the tree. Thus suppose that in some position there are, say, five capturing moves. The capture reordering routine shuffles these moves in with the first five noncapturing moves on the moves list as follows. A capture of the piece just moved at the last ply is placed at the top, except at ply 1, where this is done only if the capture is a recapturing move since the opponent most likely is not giving material away. Captures by non-Pawns in the opponent's territory are usually interchanged with noncapturing moves. No capture is ever reordered down the moves list to a point where it would not be considered due to the fanout of the tree at that level. For example, a capture at a level in the tree where the fanout is, say, eight would never be moved to the ninth position on the moves list.

Special Reordering. After the capture reordering has been completed, a special reordering routine again reorders the moves. The following special reordering is performed on the moves list at ply 1, using information stored from the *previous move*. The computer retrieves a move called SECOND BEST and seeks a match with this move. If a match is found this move is placed at the top of the moves list and the other moves are pushed down one position. SECOND BEST was calculated on the computer's previous move and is the second last move that the search thought was best as it searched the first-ply move list. If the best move happened to be at the top of this list, the move SECOND BEST will not exist. Further, even if the move SECOND BEST was found on the previous move, it may be illegal in the new position. Next, the move on the third-ply best response list that was previously calculated as being the best response to the opponent's last move is retrieved. Again, this move may not exist. If, for example, referring to Fig. X-8, the opponent makes move M_b, then move M_y is retrieved while responses to moves M_c and M_d do not exist. The same procedure is then applied to this move as was applied to SECOND BEST.

On moves lists at plies 2–5, special reordering is also performed. First, the most recent refutation is retrieved, a match is sought, and, if one is found, this move is placed at the top of the moves list. Next, at plies 2 and 4, the move presently on the principal continuation at ply 2 is retrieved, a match is sought, and, if one is found, this move is placed

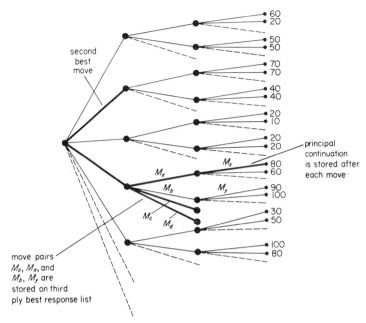

second
best
move

principal
continuation
is stored after
each move·

M_a

M_x

M_b

M_y

M_c

M_d

move pairs
M_a, M_x, and
M_b, M_y are
stored on third
ply best response list

Fig. X-8. *A tree illustrating moves stored for special reordering on the next* move.

at the top of the moves list. Similarly, at plies 3 and 5, the move at ply 1 in the principal continuation is retrieved, etc.

Midsearch Reordering. When the third move at ply 1 is ready for consideration a midsearch reordering routine is applied to the ply-1 moves list. Specifically, the move at the third ply in the present principal continuation is retrieved and a match is sought with those moves that remain on the ply-1 moves list. If a match is found, this move is placed at the top of the list of remaining moves and all others are pushed down one position. If no match is found the most recent refutation is retrieved and again a match is sought, etc. This reordering is actually performed just prior to the selection of each ply-1 move, starting with the third move. Thus the moves list at ply 1 is constantly being reexamined and reordered as the search progresses.

In general, the reordering routines allow the program to take advantage of good moves found during the tree search. Good moves found deep in the tree are often good bets to try near the root of the tree; similarly, good moves found near the root of the tree are worth considering at deeper levels of the tree.

G.   Processing at Terminal Nodes

Once it has been decided that a node is a terminal node, the scoring of the position begins. The *Scoring Routine* is composed of 17 subprograms, each of which gives credit for having certain features present on the board. Some of these features are given credit only during certain stages of the game. The score of a position consists of two vector components. The first, the *material* component, is the sum of terms 1 and 14; the second component is the sum of the other terms. Terms 1 and 14 involve material on the board. They were separated from the other terms to ensure that material is never exchanged for other nonmaterial gains.

Term 1: Board Material (Component 1)

The dominant factor in most positions is material. At this point in the development of computer chess programming a level of sophistication has not been reached where, except in the simplest of cases, a sacrifice in material can be wisely made in return for a long-term advantage. Thus to lose a piece is to be behind. Most opening gambits are beyond the understanding of even the better chess playing programs. Thus OSTRICH never knowingly sacrifices material. The values given to the pieces are: Pawn = 1 unit, Knight = Bishop = 3 units, Rook = 5 units, Queen = 9 units, and King = 200 units.

Term 2: Material Ratio (Component 2)

This term encourages trading pieces when ahead and not trading pieces when behind. This is generally good chess strategy, but it can sometimes lead to foolish moves. For example, in a Bishop, Pawn, and King versus Pawn and King end game it would most likely be a mistake for the side with the Bishop to encourage a Pawn trade unless necessary to prevent the opponent's Pawn from Queening. The material ratio term gives a 100-point bonus to the side with the most material if an even exchange of material has taken place on the branches of the tree under investigation. If material is even, the term has no effect. However, if one side is ahead by a Pawn or more the term takes effect.

Term 3: Castling (Component 2)

A 600-point bonus is awarded for a King-side castling move. A Queen-side castling move is worth 300 points.

Term 4: Board Control (Component 2)

Control of a square is defined as the ability of a piece to capture a hypothetical enemy piece on that square. Control of any of the four center squares is worth 12 points; control over the next ring of squares (QB3, Q3, K3, KB3, KB4, KB5, KB6, K6, Q6, QB6, QB5, QB4) is worth 7 points; the next ring is worth 4 points; while no credit is given for control of squares on the four sides of the board. Control over each square near the opponent's King is also given 12 points credit.

Term 5: Tempi (Component 2)

An important chess concept is that of tempo. To give the program some sense of tempo, this routine deducts 200 points from the score of any side which commits any of these time wasters:

(a) Moving the same piece twice in the opening.
(b) Moving a King or Rook before castling.
(c) Moving a piece back to where it came from on the last move.
(d) Moving a piece to a square in two moves to which it could move in one.

Term 6: Early Queen Moves (Component 2)

OSTRICH gives a 400-point penalty for any Queen move before the eighth move of a game. Without this penalty OSTRICH is too eager to bring the Queen out into the action before the normal development of minor pieces has been completed.

Term 7: Blocking Unadvanced Center Pawns (Component 2)

A position may become hopelessly cramped by placing minor pieces in front of unadvanced center pawns. OSTRICH is discouraged from doing this by a subroutine that deducts 470 points for blocking an unadvanced King or Queen pawn.

Term 8: Development of Minor Pieces (Component 2)

Rapid development of Knights, Bishops, and center Pawns is encouraged by this routine, which assesses a penalty of 140 points for each unmoved Knight, Bishop, and center Pawn.

Term 9: Pawns in Center (Component 2)

A 50–point bonus is given for each Pawn on K4 or Q4; a 70-point bonus is given for each pawn on K5 or Q5.

Term 10: Pawn Structure (Component 2)

Pawns are given credit for advancement (10 points); a 20-point penalty is given for each doubled pawn; isolated pawns are penalized 400 points.

Term 11: Passed Pawns (Component 2)

Passed pawns are given increasing credit as they approach the eighth rank. If there are no pieces other than Pawns and Kings on the board, a passed Pawn on the seventh rank is worth 1600 points, on the sixth rank 1000 points, on the fifth rank 700 points, on the fourth rank 300 points, on the third rank 200 points, and on the second rank 100 points. If there are other types of pieces on the board, then a passed Pawn on the seventh rank is worth 700 points, the sixth rank 400 points, the fifth rank 340 points, the fourth rank 40 points, the third rank 100 points, and the second rank 40 points.

Term 12: King Defense (Component 2)

This subroutine was added to encourage the program to keep some warriors at home to defend the King when the opponent is applying pressure. If the number of enemy non-Pawns in the King's sector (that quadrant of the board in which the King is located) exceeds the number of defenders, a 75–point penalty is introduced for each excess piece.

Term 13: Doubled Rooks, Bishop Pairs (Component 2)

Two Rooks on the same column are worth 150 points. If one side has a pair of Bishops while the other side does not, a 150-point bonus is given.

Term 14: Extended Trade Analyzer (Component 1)

This subroutine begins by finding out whether the piece that moved at the last ply is under attack. If so, the score is adjusted as follows: (1) If the number of defenders is zero, then the score is reduced by the value of the attacked piece; (2) otherwise, a simulated sequence of trades is carried out on the square and the score is adjusted based on the material exchange. This subroutine was introduced just prior to the 1972 ACM Tournament and is based on the "follow the action" philosophy and the observation that immediate captures refute a large percentage of all moves.

Term 15: King against Pawns (Component 2)

This routine takes effect after move 30 of the game. It gives 200 points credit if the King is within one square of an enemy Pawn. This algorithm encourages the King to move towards an enemy Pawn with the goal of eventually capturing it.

Term 16: "Knight on the Rim is Dim" (Component 2)

This old chess proverb has been included as a scoring factor. A Knight on column 0 or 7 receives a penalty of 40 points.

Term 17: Attack Encourager (Component 2)

Moves at ply 1 that put an opponent's piece on en prise are given a 40-point bonus. This term gives the program an aggressive spirit.

H.   The Gamma Algorithm

The *gamma algorithm* causes certain nodes in the tree to be considered terminal nodes. Unlike the alpha-beta algorithm, it is possible that the gamma algorithm will cause the search to arrive at a nonoptimal principal continuation. In particular, it will cause the search to miss those continuations that involve a sacrifice at ply i that is not recovered before ply $i + 4$.

The gamma algorithm is included in the tests that determine whether a node is a terminal or nonterminal node. For example, suppose the search has reached node P_i in Fig. X-9. The algorithm specifies the following:

(1) Determine the material score (term 1 of the scoring function) of node P_i.

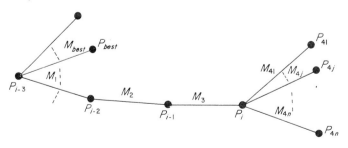

Fig. X-9. *Partial tree illustrating the gamma algorithm.*

(2) Compare this score with the material score of the node P_{best} that follows by making the best move M_{best} found so far at node P_{i-3}.

(3) If the score of P_i implies that the move sequence $M_1M_2M_3$ is worse than the move M_{best}, then stop search at node P_i; i.e., consider P_i a terminal node and assign it the score determined in step (1). Otherwise continue with the other tests.

The philosophy behind the algorithm is as follows: If move sequence $M_1M_2M_3$ leads to a worse position than does move M_{best}, then the probability is small that a deeper search will change the situation. Certainly it is highly unlikely to be changed by searching one additional ply, since the opponent is likely to have at least one move, say, M_{4j} for which the move sequence $M_1M_2M_3M_{4j}$ leads to a position P_{4j} which is worse than position P_{best}. Thus, rather than spend time examining successors of positions P_i if move sequence $M_1M_2M_3$ is worse than move M_{best}, it appears more worthwhile to examine other moves in the tree—especially additional moves at early plies in the tree.

The First World Computer Chess Championship (Stockholm, 1974)

Thirteen programs recently took part in the First World Computer Chess Championship held in Stockholm, Sweden, August 5–8, 1974. The four-round Swiss-system tournament, held in the Hotel Birger Jarl, was part of the triennial IFIP-74 Congress. Competing were four programs from the USA (CHESS 4.0, CHAOS, TECH II, and OSTRICH), three from England (MASTER, BEAL, and A16CHS), one from Austria (FRANTZ), one from Canada (RIBBIT), one from Hungary (PAPA), one from Norway (FREEDOM), one from Switzerland (TELL), and one from the USSR (KAISSA). Computers were tied into the Birger Jarl from remote locations in Sweden and other European countries; a voice line, direct to Moscow's Institute of Control Science, linked KAISSA to the hotel. Two computers were at the site of the tournament, a Data General Nova 2 and a Hewlett-Packard HP 2100.

KAISSA won the tournament, winning all four of its games. CHESS 4.0, RIBBIT, and CHAOS each earned three points. The tournament rules for breaking ties (involving the length of the games played) eliminated CHAOS and set up a play-off game for second place between CHESS 4.0 and RIBBIT. The play-off was won by CHESS 4.0 (See Table A1-1.) Since KAISSA and CHESS 4.0 did not meet in the tournament and since there was considerable interest in how they would do against one another, a friendly one-game match was played on the day following the conclusion of the tournament. KAISSA, having a won game most of the way, let its lead disappear and settled for a draw. The game ended with KAISSA having a Rook, Knight, and King on the board and CHESS 4.0 having only a Rook and King.

It is interesting to observe that the two top programs, KAISSA and CHESS 4.0, are both essentially implementations of Shannon's type-A strategy. The third place finisher, RIBBIT, while not strictly a type-A program, searches a very large tree. Of the first six finishers, CHAOS performs the most selective search, examining of the order of 4500 terminal positions per three-minute move. These programs are in sharp contrast with the recently developed experimental program of Berliner, CAPS-II [1].

Date: 8/6/74   Round: 2   Board: 1

WHITE: *CHAOS*   BLACK: *CHESS 4.0*

Queen's Gambit Accepted

An analysis of this game by David Levy appears in the *Communications of the ACM* [2]. CHAOS makes an unusually clever sacrifice on move 16, plays good tactical chess for the next 30 moves, and enters the end game on move 47 with a Rook, two Pawns, and a King to CHESS 4.0's single Pawn and King. The end game illustrates the difficulties programs have with this part of the game. CHAOS finds it hard to concentrate on the simple theme—to advance a Pawn that is free to promote.

1 P–Q4 (B)	P–Q4 (B)	6 Q–K2 (B)	P–QR3 (B)
2 P–QB4 (B)	P × P (B)	7 O–O (B)	P–QN4 (B)
3 N–KB3 (B)	N–KB3 (B)	8 B–N3 (B)	B–N2 (B)
4 P–K3 (B)	P–K3 (B)	9 R–Q1 (B)	. . .
5 B × P (B)	P–B4 (B)		

The authors of CHAOS have modified their book and it is different than that used at the Fourth United States Computer Chess Championship. (See CHAOS versus CHESS 4.0, pp. 149–151.)

9 . . .	N(N1)–Q2 (B)	12 N × P(Q4) (B)	Q–N1 (B)
10 N–B3 (B)	B–Q3 (B)	13 P–N3 (B)	P–N5 (211)
11 P–K4 (B)	P × P (B)		

CHESS 4.0 has no reply to 13 P–N3 in its book. Its move, 13 . . . , P–N5 will also take CHAOS out of its book. CHAOS expected 13 . . . , O–O,

Fig. A1-1. *Position after 15 . . . , B–N3.*

but CHESS 4.0 is more interested in winning White's King's Pawn. CHAOS, having built up a large time surplus, will play quite slowly for the next few moves.

14 N–R4 (425)   B × P(K5) (61)   15 P–B3 (203)   B–N3 (198)

(See Fig A1-1.)

16 N × P (587)   . . .

CHAOS predicts 16 . . . , P × N, 17 Q × P(K6)+, B–K2, 18 B–K3, after examining 17,508 positions in about ten minutes. CHAOS feels that the loss in material is more than compensated for by gains in positional factors. The move at ply 5 was selected for positional considerations. CHAOS examined six moves at the first ply. It tried in order: 16 N–QB6, 16 B–KN5, 16 B–Q2, 16 B–K3, 16 N × P, and finally 16 B–KB4.

16 . . .   P × N (66)   17 Q × P(K6)+ (288)   . . .

CHAOS examines 6108 terminal positions and sees the continuation 17 . . . , B–K2, 18 R–K1, Q–K1, 19 B–KB4. The move at the last ply is again selected because of positional considerations and not in anticipation of 20 B–B7 attacking Black's Queen.

17 . . .   B–K2 (62)   20 R(R1)–Q1 (241)   R–R2 (70)
18 R–K1 (443)   Q–Q1 (126)   21 R–QB1 (754)   . . .
19 B–KB4 (106) K–B1 (36)

CHAOS deliberated over twelve minutes. Levy suggests that "21 B–Q6, N–KN1, 22 N–B5 wins at once; e.g., 22 . . . , N × N, 23 B × B+, Q × B, 24 Q–B8+, etc. The next move threatens 22 R–B8!, Q × R, 23 Q × B mate."

21 . . .	N–KN1 (79)	25 N–B5 (155)	B–B4 (187)
22 R(B1)–Q1 (393)	P–QR4 (48)	26 P–N4 (130)	Q–K1 (133)
23 B–Q6 (89)	B × B (131)	27 B–R4 (173)	. . .
24 Q × B+ (139)	N–K2 (158)		

Levy remarks that CHESS 4.0 is in serious trouble! "Both Knights are pinned, the King's Rook is worthless, the Queen's Rook and Queen are passive, the Bishop is lost. In contrast, all of White's forces are bearing down on the suffering Black King." (See Fig. A1-2.)

27 . . .	P–N6 (70)	30 R × Q (291)	R–R3 (551)
28 P × B (91)	P × P (99)	31 N × R (246)	Q–Q1 (54)
29 B × N (198)	P–R8=Q (526)	32 K–B2 (52)	. . .

This is a strange move. There are five moves that should bring the game to a fast end: 32 P–B6, 32 R × P, 32 R(R1)–B1, 32 N–B5, and 32 N–B7.

| 32 . . . | K–B2 (97) | 34 Q × N+ (197) | . . . |
| 33 Q–K6+ (56) | K–B1 (1) | | |

CHAOS ignores 34 P–B6, evidently feeling that the forthcoming exchanges are sufficient to give it a won position.

| 34 . . . | Q × Q (67) | 36 N–B5 (280) | R–QN1 (175) |
| 35 R × Q (95) | K × R (59) | | |

CHESS 4.0, realizing that it is in a lost position, offers to exchange Pawns on this move and on move 38.

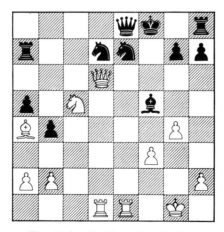

Fig. A1-2. *Position after 27 B–R4.*

37 R × P (91)	R × P+ (57)	42 R–K5 (263)	R–B8 (208)
38 K–N3 (218)	P–N3 (274)	43 R–N5 (276)	K–B2 (228)
39 P × P (120)	P × P (112)	44 B–K6+ (113)	K–B3 (171)
40 R–R6 (75)	R–QB7 (65)	45 P–R4 (306)	R × N (68)
41 R–K6+ (259)	K–B1 (64)	46 R × R (13)	K × B (59)

The win looks simple, but CHAOS requires another 33 moves.

47 R–KN5 (23)	K–B3 (218)	57 R–QB8 (151)	K–N4 (60)
48 K–N4 (22)	K–B2 (163)	58 P–R5 (66)	K–N3 (405)
49 R–QB5 (38)	K–K3 (85)	59 R–B1 (143)	K–N4 (54)
50 K–N5 (72)	K–Q3 (158)	60 P–R6 (206)	K–R5 (63)
51 R–R5 (187)	K–B3 (98)	61 R–QN1 (250)	K–R6 (320)
52 P–B4 (339)	K–N3 (191)	62 P–B5 (250)	K–R7 (371)
53 R–R1 (243)	K–B4 (61)	63 R–N8 (26)	K–R6 (17)
54 R–Q1 (138)	K–N5 (69)	64 P–B6 (232)	K–R5 (339)
55 K × P (183)	K–B6 (86)	65 R–N7 (9)	. . .
56 R–Q8 (391)	K–N5 (67)		

CHAOS sees forced mate in seven. On move 67 it sees forced mate in nine, and on move 69 it sees forced mate in seven. However, CHAOS does not save the principal continuation for use on later moves and gets sidetracked on moves 66, 68, and 70.

65 . . .	K–R4 (304)	73 R–N8 (211)	K–R4 (292)
66 R–N8 (199)	K–R5 (22)	74 K–N8 (166)	K–R5 (208)
67 R–N1 (8)	K–R6 (315)	75 P–R7 (379)	K–R4 (20)
68 R–N7 (272)	K–R5 (16)	76 P–R8=Q (7)	K–R5 (3)
69 R–N8 (4)	K–R4 (346)	77 Q–R4+ (1)	K–R4 (3)
70 K–N7 (235)	K–R5 (281)	78 Q–QN4+ (1)	K–R3 (1)
71 R–N7 (151)	K–R4 (248)	79 Q–QR4 mate (1)	
72 R–N2 (207)	K–R5 (459)		

The amount of time that each move required was recorded for both sides by OSTRICH. The number of terminal positions scored by OSTRICH on each move is also indicated.

Date: 8/9/74   Round: 4   Board: 1

WHITE: *OSTRICH*   BLACK: *KAISSA*

The next game begins rather tamely, with KAISSA gaining a slight positional advantage when OSTRICH triples its Pawns on 11 P × P.

KAISSA, however, plays somewhat imprecisely and fails to capitalize on its small advantage. OSTRICH gradually recovers, and then on move 19 KAISSA errs badly allowing OSTRICH to win the exchange of a Rook for a Knight. OSTRICH maintains the lead until move 40, having forced mate on two different occasions, but missing them both because they require deep analysis to see that a sacrifice is correct. The mating opportunities for OSTRICH come on moves 35 and 39. KAISSA gains the upper hand on move 40, gradually increases its advantage, and finally mates OSTRICH on move 67.

Reti's Opening

1 N–KB3 (12)*	P–K3 (11)	4 P–K3 (110)	B–K2 (7)
(956)**		(7949)	
2 P–Q4 (38)	N–KB3 (6)	5 N–B3 (82)	B–N5 (334)
(2614)		(5459)	
3 B–N5 (53)	P–Q4 (6)		
(4045)			

KAISSA plays from a book for the first four moves but is not prepared to respond to OSTRICH's fifth move. KAISSA's move, which took over six minutes to decide, wastes a tempo.

6 B × N (107)	B × N+ (59)	9 O–O (269)	O–O (15)
(7432)		(18,152)	
7 P × B (43)	Q × B (19)	10 Q–Q2 (414)	N–B3 (248)
(3383)		(27,644)	
8 B–Q3 (55)	P–B4 (287)		
(3976)			

KAISSA correctly develops the Knight, leaving the Queen's Bishop's Pawn undefended. OSTRICH is given the opportunity to capture the Pawn, but by doing so it must accept the liability of tripled isolated Pawns. OSTRICH will bite, giving KAISSA a clear positional advantage. KAISSA will fail, however, to capitalize on the advantage.

11 P × P (252) (16,588)   Q–K2 (35)

Better for KAISSA is 11 . . . , R–Q1.

12 P–B4 (285) (17,430)   . . .

* Time in seconds.
** Number of terminal positions.

OSTRICH plays correctly here.

12 . . .	P × P (159)	14 Q–Q3 (92)	R–Q1 (187)
13 B × P(B4) (250)	Q × P (19)	(5499)	
(15,417)		15 Q–K4 (112)	P–QN4 (399)
		(6558)	

This move gives KAISSA's Bishop a square on which to develop, but also chases White's Bishop to a better square.

16 B–Q3 (269)	P–B4 (304)	17 Q–KR4 (185)	P–K4 (318)
(17,008)		(10,824)	

KAISSA is threatening 18 . . . , P–K5.

18 P–K4 (219)	P–B5 (82)	19 R(B1)–K1 (263)	. . .
(13,197)		(16,523)	

This is the first of several Rook moves by OSTRICH that are pointless.

19 . . .   B–N2 (308)

KAISSA requires six minutes to blunder!

20 N–N5 (76)	P–KR3 (267)	22 N × R (75)	R × N (45)
(4050)		(4075)	
21 N–K6 (73)	Q–N3 (141)	23 P–QR4 (361)	. . .
(4255)		(21,038)	

This is not best. More active is 23 R(R1)–N1.

23 . . .	P–N5 (195)	25 R(R1)–Q1 (111)	N–Q5 (186)
		(6483)	
24 B–B4+ (32)	K–R1 (168)	26 R–QB1 (297)	. . .
(1759)		(18,231)	

A second weak move by the Rooks is made; 26 Q–K7 is much better.

26 . . .	B–B3 (227)	30 Q–KB7 (48)	Q–B4 (243)
		(2600)	
27 P–QB3 (158)	P × P (76)	31 R–Q3 (56)	N–Q5 (164)
(9754)		(3061)	
28 R × P (72)	B × P(R5) (143)	32 B–Q5 (98)	. . .
(4051)		(5651)	
29 Q–K7 (167)	N–B3 (59)		
(9698)			

KAISSA, down a Rook for a Knight, has the opportunity to draw in this position, but most likely is not able to see it: 32 . . . , N–K7+, 33 K–B1, B–N4, and if 34 R–Q2, N–N6+, etc. No better for White is 34 K × N or 34 R–KR3.

32 . . .	B–N4 (271)	34 K–R1 (102)	Q × P (208)
		(6504)	
33 R–KR3 (343)	N–K7+ (105)	35 R–Q1 (77)	. . .
(19,543)		(5087)	

(See Fig. A1-3.) OSTRICH misses a forced mate! But it involves a sacrifice and a deep analysis: 35 R × P+, P × R, 36 Q–B6+, K–R2, 37 Q–K7+, K–N6, 38 Q–B7+, K–N5, 39 Q–N7+, K–R4, 40 B–B7+, K–R5, 41 Q × P(R6)+, K–N5, 42 B–K6 mate! Sad to say for OSTRICH, it is not able to see the 15-ply analysis.

35 . . .	Q–N3 (198)	37 B–K6 (109)	R–Q1 (25)
		(6509)	
36 R–QN1 (174)	R–QB1 (232)	38 Q–N6 (94)	Q–N2 (227)
(10,690)		(5560)	

(See Fig. A1-4.) If OSTRICH plays 39 B–B5, mate is eventually forced. For example, 39 B–B5, K–N1 (Black can stall the mate for several moves by giving a few ineffective checks), 40 R × P, threatening 41 R–R8+. If 40 . . . , K–B1, 41 R–R8+, K–K2, 42 Q–K6 mate. Thus including the two stalling checks, OSTRICH must search to a depth of 11 ply to see the forced mate. However, the version of OSTRICH used in the tournament did not include the gamma algorithm and stopped search on all sequences

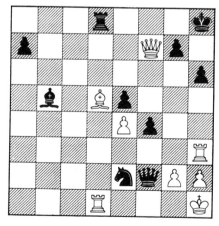

Fig. A1-3.   *Position after 34 . . . , Q × P. OSTRICH has forced mate in 15 Ply.*

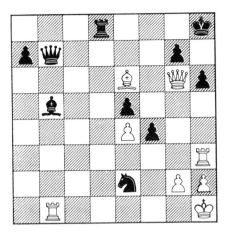

Fig. A1-4. *Position after 38 . . . , Q–N2. OSTRICH has forced a mate in 11 ply.*

after at most six ply (see Chapter X for a description of OSTRICH). To see that 39 R × P+ gives OSTRICH a larger lead requires a seven-ply analysis.

| 39 Q–B5 (166) | Q–QB2 (240) | 40 R–R4 (87) | N–Q5 (245) |
| (10,270) | | (5075) | |

KAISSA has recovered and will go to the offensive. Both sides were in slight time trouble. KAISSA's move 40 was made with less than two minutes on its clock.

41 Q–R3 (141)	N × B (87)	44 Q–B5 (101)	B–K7 (176)
(8498)		(6449)	
42 Q × N (112)	B–Q6 (99)	45 R–R1 (172)	P–QR4 (498)
(8027)		(11,719)	
43 R–N1 (281)	B–B5 (72)		
(17,257)			

KAISSA finds the road to victory. It meditated for eight minutes on this move.

46 Q–N6 (172)	P–R5 (290)	50 Q × Q (74)	R × Q (31)
(11,833)		(5130)	
47 R–K1 (135)	B–B5 (287)	51 R–R3 (151)	P–R7 (11)
(9337)		(13,484)	
48 R–R1 (245)	P–R6 (277)	52 R–QB1 (294)	R–Q5 (31)
(16,721)		(28,174)	
49 R–QN1 (215)	Q–Q3 (307)	53 R(R3)–QB3	R × P (480)
(14,649)		(217) (19,872)	

TABLE AI-1 Final Standings of the First World Computer Chess Championship

	Program, authors, computer, location of computer	Affiliation, country	Round				Points
			1	2	3	4	
1.	KAISSA; Mikhail Domskoy; ICL 4/70; Institute of Control Science	Institute of Control Sciences, USSR	W7	W5	W4	W6	4
2.	CHESS 4.0; David Slate, Larry Atkin; CDC 6600; Stockholm	Northwestern Univ., USA	W3	L4	W6	W5	3[a]
3.	RIBBIT; Jim Parry, Ron Hansen, Russell Crook; Honeywell 6060 ASEA; Vasteras, Sweden	Univ. of Waterloo, Canada	L2	W10	W13	W9	3
4.	CHAOS; Ira Ruben, Fred Swartz, Joe Winograd, Victor Berman, William Toikka; UNIVAC 1110; Bergen, Norway	UNIVAC, USA	W10	W2	L1	W8	3
5.	TECH II; Alan Baisley; PDP 10; Stockholm	MIT, USA	W8	L1	W7	L2	2
6.	OSTRICH; George Arnold, Monroe Newborn; Data General Nova 2; at tournament site	Columbia Univ., USA	W11	W9	L2	L1	2
7.	FRANTZ; Gerhard Wolf; UNIVAC 494; Stockholm	Rechenzentrum Graz, Austria	L1	W13	L5	W12	2
8.	MASTER; Peter Kent, J. A. Birmingham; IBM 370/195; Chilton, England	Atlas Computer Lab., England	L5	W12	W11	L4	2
9.	BEAL; Don Beal; CDC 6400; London	Queen Mary College, England	Bye	L6	W12	L3	**2**
10.	FREEDOM; Nils Barricelli; CDC Cyber 74; Kjeller, Norway	Oslo Univ., Norway	L4	L3	Bye	D11	1½
11.	TELL; Johann Joss; HP 2100; at tournament site	ETH, Switzerland	L6	Bye	L8	D10	1½
12.	A16CHS; Robert Prinsen; GCS–Alpha 16; Hounslow, England	Interscan Data Systems, England	W13	L8	L9	L7	1
13.	PAPA; G. Rajna, P. Almasy; CDC Cyber 73; Atomenergi, Studsvik, Sweden	Univ. of Budapest, Hungary	L12	L7	L3	Bye	1

[a] Won play-off game with RIBBIT for second place.

54 R–R1 (160) (15,916)	R–Q5 (81)	61 K–N1 (139) (11,599)	P–K7 (14)
55 R × B (119) (9663)	R × R (32)	62 K–B2 (38) (3311)	R–Q8 (17)
56 P–N3 (69) (6769)	P–B6 (45)	63 R–B8+ (24) (1854)	K–R2 (13)
57 P–R3 (68) (6386)	R–B7 (48)	64 K × P(B3) (87) (6363)	P–K8=Q (330)
58 R–Q1 (62) (5992)	R–Q7 (103)	65 R–B2 (343) (29,119)	R–Q6+ (58)
59 R–QB1 (96) (7683)	P–K5 (107)	66 K–B4 (173) (14,631)	P–N4+ (22)
60 P–N4 (335) (32,434)	P–K6 (25)	67 K–B5 (1) (1)	R–KB6 mate

References

[1] Berliner, Hans, "Chess as Problem Solving: The Development of a Tactics Analyzer." Ph.D. Dissertation, Carnegie–Mellon Univ., Pittsburgh, Pennsylvania, 1974.
[2] Mittman, Benjamin, First World Computer Chess Championship at IFIP Congress 74 Stockholm, August 5–8, *Commun. ACM*, October, 604–605, 1974.

Basic Data on Computers Involved in Computer Chess Games

Twenty-four different computers were used by the programs whose games are recorded in this book. Their capabilities are described briefly in Table A-1. Which of them is best suited for a chess program is hard to say. Speed, which seems to be the most important factor, is often difficult to measure. For example, most of the newer computers execute several instructions simultaneously, and thus to say that two computers perform an addition in, say, 1 μsec is not sufficient information to allow one to conclude that the two computers process at the same speed. A large high-speed memory would seem to be an asset, but no chess program needs more than about 128K words—a relatively modest amount for the newer larger computers. More difficult to evaluate is the effectiveness of the instruction set or the effectiveness of the higher-level languages and their compilers.

Perhaps in the future there will exist special-purpose computers to play chess or special hardware modules that can be attached to a general-purpose computer to facilitate its ability to play chess. There may also exist computers that execute tree-searching programs in a highly parallel mode—perhaps with 1000 processing units, each searching a different path in the tree, feeding information to each other and to one main processing unit that is controlling the show!

TABLE A2-1[a]

Computer[b]	Year of intro- duction	Word size (bits)	Memory size (thousands of words)	Speed (μsec) MCT[c]	AT[d]
USA					
Burroughs B5500	1964	48	4–32	4	4
Data General Nova 800	1971	16	4–32	0.8	0.8
Control Data 6400	1966	60	32–131	1	0.6
Control Data 6600	1964	60	32–131	1	0.3
Hewlett-Packard HP 3000	1971	16	24–64	0.98	
Honeywell 635	1965	32	65–262	1	1.9
IBM 704	1956	36	4	12	84
IBM 7090	1958	36	32	2.18	4.36
IBM 360/65	1966	32	32–256	0.75	1.3
IBM 360/91	1967	32	128–256	0.75	0.18
IBM 370/145	1970	32	32–128	0.2	0.2
IBM 370/155	1970	32	64–512	0.115	0.115
Digital Equipment PDP-6	1964	36	16–262	1.75	4.4
Digital Equipment PDP-10	1967	36	262	1	2.5
Digital Equipment PDP 11/45	1971	16	4–128	0.3	0.3
MANIAC I	1952	40	4	90	
UNIVAC 1106	1970	36	65–252	1.5	1.5
UNIVAC 1108	1965	36	65–252	0.75	0.75
UNIVAC 494	1966	30	65–131	0.75	0.75
UNIVAC 418 III	1969	18	32–131	0.75	1.5
Varian 620/i	1965	18	4–32	1.8	3.6
Xerox Data Systems 940	1966	24	32	1.75	3.5
Foreign					
ICL 4/70 (England)	1969	36	16–256	1.1	1.1
ICL 1909/5 (England)	1965	24	4	6	18
M-20 (USSR)	1959	45	4	50	

[a] Data from the following sources: *Computer Characteristics Rev.*, Keydata Corporation, Watertown, Massachusetts (1969–1972); *Auerbach Computer Technology Repts.*, Auerbach Information, Inc., Philadelphia, Pennsylvania (1972); "Computers 1971–1981," Vol. II. Center for Technological and Interdisciplinary Forecasting, Tel Aviv University, Tel Aviv (1971); Bell, C. Gordon, and Newell, Allen, "Computer Structures: Readings and Examples." McGraw-Hill, New York (1971); Rosen, Saul, Electronic computers: A historical survey, *Computing Surveys*, pp. 7–36, ACM, March (1969); "Computer Yearbook and Directory." American Data Processing, Inc., Detroit, Michigan (1966).

[b] This list does not include computers of programs that participated in the First World Computer Chess Championship described in Appendix I.

[c] MCT = memory cycle time.

[d] AT = average time to add two integers. Some computers are able to carry out several additions simultaneously, and thus in some cases AT < MCT.

Rules Used in the Fourth United States Computer Chess Championship

1. The tournament is a four-round Swiss-system tournament with trophies to be awarded to the winner and runner-up.

2. Games begin 1 p.m. Sunday, August 26; 7:30 p.m., August 26; 7:30 p.m., August 27; and 7:30 p.m. August 28. A team may ask for a 30-minute delay if it is having technical difficulties.

3. Unless otherwise specified below, rules of play are identical to those of regular "human" tournament play. If a point is in question, the tournament director has the authority to make the final decision.

4. Games are played at a speed of 40 moves per player in the first two hours and then 10 moves every 30 minutes thereafter.

5. The tournament director has the right to adjudicate a game after six hours of total elapsed time.

6. If a team encounters technical difficulties (machine failure, communications failure or error, or program failure) during the course of a game, the tournament director may allow them to stop their clock for as long as necessary, but not to exceed 20 minutes, in order to restore their system. At the end of the 20 minutes, their clock will be started again. The tournament director may grant a team permission to stop their clock at most three times during the course of a game.

7. There is no manual adjustment of program parameters during the

course of a game. In the case of program failures, program parameters must be reset to their most recent values if it is at all posible. Information regarding castling status, *en passant* status, etc., may be typed in after a failure. If at any time during the progress of a game, the computer asks for the time remaining on either its or its opponent's clock, this information may be provided. However, the computer must initiate the request for information.

8. At the end of each game, each team is expected to turn in a game listing along with a record of the CPU time required for each move. A record of initial settings on fanout parameters and time control parameters must also be recorded.

9. Each team must include the principal author of the program that they are using or they must have the author's permission to use the program.

10. There are no restrictions on the hardware facilities.

Index

A   5
B   6
C   7
D   8
E   9
F   0
G   1
H   2
I   3
J   4